EUROPE AND JAPAN
CHANGING RELATIONSHIPS SINCE 1945

Europe and Japan

CHANGING RELATIONSHIPS SINCE 1945

Edited by

Gordon Daniels

and

Reinhard Drifte

Paul Norbury Publications
Woodchurch, Ashford, Kent

EUROPE AND JAPAN: CHANGING RELATIONSHIPS SINCE 1945

PAUL NORBURY PUBLICATIONS LTD
Woodchurch, Ashford, Kent, England

First published 1986
© Programme for Strategic and International
Security Studies (PSIS), Geneva, 1986

All rights reserved. No part of this publication
may be reproduced, stored in a retrieval system,
or transmitted in any form or by any means
without prior permission of the copyright
owners. All enquiries should be addressed to the
publishers.

ISBN 0-904404-44-7

The publishers are grateful to the Japan Foundation, Tokyo,
for their support in the making of this book.

British Library Cataloguing in Publication Data

Europe and Japan changing relationships since 1945.
1. Europe——Foreign relations——Japan   2. Japan
——Foreign relations——Europe   3. Europe——
Foreign relations——1945-   4. Japan——Foreign
relations——1945-
I. Daniels, Gordon   II. Drifte, R.
327.4052   D1065.J3

ISBN 0-904404-44-7

This book has been set in 10 on 11 point Plantin Roman
by Visual Typesetting, Harrow.

Printed in Great Britain by A. Wheaton & Co. Ltd, Exeter

Contents

PREFACE 7

CONTRIBUTORS 8

FOREWORD 9

PART I EUROPE AND JAPAN: THE HISTORICAL SETTING

1. Japan in the Post-War World – Between Europe and 12
   the United States
   GORDON DANIELS
2. Political Development, Decision-Making and Foreign 23
   Policy in Modern Japan
   ISHIDA TAKESHI

PART II EURO-JAPANESE RELATIONS: THE CONTEMPORARY SCENE
3. The Economic and Non-Economic Dimensions of Euro-Japanese 31
   Relations
   ENDYMION WILKINSON
4. Psychological Aspects of Euro-Japanese Trade Frictions: 48
   A Japanese Viewpoint
   YOSHIMORI MASARU
5. Japanese Security Policy and European Security 59
   REINHARD DRIFTE

PART III JAPAN, EUROPE AND THE SUPERPOWERS
6. Japanese-Soviet Relations in the Contemporary World 69
   JOACHIM GLAUBITZ
7. Regional policies in Europe and East Asia 79
   WOLF MENDL

PART IV CONCLUSIONS
8. Euro-Japanese Relations: Realities and Prospects 92
   REINHARD DRIFTE

PART V DATA AND DOCUMENTS
Japan-Europe-USA: August 1945-December 1985 A Brief Chronology 106
STATISTICAL TABLES
TABLE 1 EC/Japan bilateral trade (Eurostat), 1973-83 109
TABLE 2 EC/Japan bilateral trade (Ministry of Finance, Japan), 109
  1973-83
TABLE 3 Japanese business representatives to the 110
  United States and Europe, and US and European business
  representatives to Japan for long-term business stays

DOCUMENTS

DOCUMENT 1 Motion for a Resolution on Trade Relations 111
  between the EC and Japan agreed by the Committee
  on External Economic Relations (of the European
  Parliament). Agreed 13 May 1981.

DOCUMENT 2	External Economic Measures Agreed by the Ministerial Conference for Economic Measures (Japan), 16 December 1981.	114
DOCUMENT 3	Luncheon Address to the Nihon Press Club by Gaston E. Thorn, President of the Commission of the European Communities, 11 May 1984. (*Extracts*)	115
DOCUMENT 4	Statement of Prime Minister Nakasone on the outline of the Action Programme, 30 July 1985.	117
DOCUMENT 5	Commission Communication to the Council — Analysis of the Relations between the Community and Japan, 15 October 1985 (*Extracts*)	119

APPENDIX 1
Prime Ministers of Japan since the restoration of Japanese sovereignty, 28 April 1952. — 122

APPENDIX 2
Presidents of the Commission of the European Economic Community (7 January 1958 – 30 June 1967) and of the European Communities, from 1 July 1967. — 122

APPENDIX 3
Japanese Ministers of Foreign Affairs since the restoration of sovereignty, 28 April 1952. — 122

APPENDIX 4
Commissioners for External Relations of the European Economic Community (January 1958 – July 1967) and of the European Communities (from 1 July 1967). — 123

APPENDIX 5
Japanese Ambassadors to the European Economic Community, the European Coal and Steel Community and Euratom (December 1959 – June 1967) and to the Commission of the European Communities (from July 1967 to January 1986)* — 123

APPENDIX 6
Heads of the European Community's delegation in Tokyo, since its opening on 31 May 1974. — 123

*Time of going to press.

Preface

This volume has developed from a workshop which I organised in May 1982 as research fellow in the Programme for Strategic and International Security Studies (PSIS) at the Graduate Institute of International Studies, Geneva. This meeting brought together European Japanologists and Japanese scholars to examine contemporary Euro-Japanese relations and the impact of superpower policies upon ties between Japan and Western Europe.

The Programme for Strategic and International Security Studies is grateful to the Japan Foundation, Tokyo, which generously supported part of the workshop and this publication. I would also like to thank the Graduate Institute of International Studies for its help in organising and hosting the workshop. Finally, I wish to thank all contributors to this volume, not only for their valuable papers (and for the time given subsequently to updating their papers, where appropriate, prior to publication), but for participating in the Geneva workshop, at considerable personal cost.

REINHARD DRIFTE

Contributors

GORDON DANIELS is Senior Lecturer in Modern Far Eastern History, Centre for Japanese Studies, University of Sheffield. He is the editor of *Europe Interprets Japan* (1984) and, in 1985, was Visiting Fellow at the Research Institute for Humanistic Studies, Kyoto University.

REINHARD DRIFTE is Assistant Director at the International Institute for Strategic Studies, London, and is author of *The Security Factor in Japan's Foreign Policy, 1945-1952* (1983) and co-author of *Japan's Quest for Comprehensive Security* (1983). He was previously Research Fellow at the Graduate Institute of International Studies, Geneva and also worked for the EC Commission.

JOACHIM GLAUBITZ is Professor at the Research Institute for International Politics and Security, Munich.

ISHIDA TAKESHI is Professor of Political Science at Chiba University, Japan. He is the author of *Japanese Society* and was formerly Professor of Politics at the Social Science Research Institute, Tokyo University.

WOLF MENDL is Reader at the Department of War Studies, King's College, London. He is author of *Western Europe and Japan Between the Superpowers* (1984).

YOSHIMORI MASARU is Professor at the International University of Japan, Niigata Prefecture. He was formerly on the staff of the University of Paris and INSEAD, Fontainebleau.

ENDYMION WILKINSON is currently stationed in Bangkok as Deputy Head of the EC Delegation to South-East Asia. His most recent book *Japan versus Europe* (Pelican, 1983) was a best-seller in Japan when first published under the title of *Misunderstanding* (1981).

NOTE: Throughout the text Japanese names are given in the Japanese style – with the family name preceding the given name.

Foreword

Although the United States opened Japan to modern diplomacy in 1854 European powers played a central role in her nineteenth-century development. She saw powerful European states as models for industrial, political and military modernisation, and her new army, navy and constitution all bore the stamp of European influence. Conversely, Japanese leaders often saw European colonial and commercial expansion as the chief threats to their own nation's growth and independence. Indeed, European imperialism provided a further significant blueprint, for Japan's own annexation of Taiwan, Korea and territory in Manchuria.

At the beginning of the twentieth-century Japan's conclusion of an alliance with one European empire, Britain, and her victory over another, Russia, also provided the ultimate indices of her emergence as a major power. Her international status was further confirmed by her participation in the European Great War and her activities in the League of Nations at Geneva.

However, in the first decades of the twentieth-century the United States began to develop as a rival focus of Japanese interest. America's annexation of Hawaii and the Philippines made her a Pacific colonial power, while her naval and commercial presence in East Asia became increasingly significant. Of almost equal importance was the establishment of Japanese immigrant communities in the United States, and the local and diplomatic tension which stemmed from racial discrimination.

Despite the rising importance of Japanese-American relations and the ending of the Anglo-Japanese alliance (1921), Europe continued to be a centre of interest for Japanese leaders. Britain, France and Holland ruled important colonies in China, South East Asia and the Pacific, and European political ideas influenced Japanese thinkers. In the 'Taisho democracy' of the 1920s British constitutional monarchy often seemed the most suitable precedent for Japan's political evolution, while European socialism inspired the activities of much of the Japanese left.

During the world recession of the 1930s European ideas continued to attract Japanese attention. To a small minority Soviet Communism appeared admirable, while military and right wing leaders saw German and Italian fascism as suitable models for national reconstruction. Indeed much right wing pressure for a new political order was based upon European ideas of 'total war', and a desire to secure the dynamism and autarky which were advocated by Hitler, Mussolini and their supporters.

Parallel with this ideological interest in Germany and Italy went important diplomatic links. Even before the creation of Japan's own one-party system in October 1940, she signed the Tripartite Pact with Rome and Berlin. This was a major element in Japanese strategy and produced growing tension with the United States.

In December 1941 Japan declared war on Britain, America and the Netherlands, and invaded their colonies in South-East Asia. In part, this strategy also stemmed from events in Western Europe. Germany's conquest of France and Holland, and her threat to invade Britain, left vast colonies ill-defended. Troubled by American economic sanctions, Japan seized this opportunity to secure new territory and important resources.

Despite the significance of the Tripartite Pact, war in the Pacific was overwhelmingly a struggle between Japan and the United States. It was American power which drove Japan to surrender and this victory temporarily severed many of Japan's links with European culture and diplomacy. In the post-war years America occupied Japan, democratised her institutions, and became an overwhelming cultural and commercial influence. Furthermore she became the overall guarantor of Japan's political and economic security. Washington encouraged Japanese reconstruction, ensured a liberal peace treaty and agreed to defend Japan against threats from abroad. Equally important was America's generous acceptance of Japanese exports, a major encouragement to her ally's growth.

In Western Europe, as in Japan, the post-war years were a time of American aid and reconstruction. But European attitudes to Japan were less sympathetic than those in the United States. Memories of wartime brutality were powerful, while decolonisation and the Cold War distracted attention from the new Japan. Indeed it was only in the 1970s when Japanese goods swept into European markets that something of the traditional momentum of Euro-Japanese relations was restored.

For Japan, faced by the danger of American restrictions Europe represented a valuable additional market. But for Europeans the success of Japanese goods seemed to threaten jobs, and the fate of governments. Consequently, Euro-Japanese relations soon became acrimonious, and recurrent crises often stirred public emotion. However, by the 1980s both parties had come to recognise that, as in earlier times, they were linked by common interests as well as conflict. Both are allied to the United States. Both live by world trade, and both fuel their economies with imported energy. With these common concerns their relations have expanded to embrace broader issues than trade, markets and unflattering images.

In the broad-ranging chapters which follow, both Europeans and Japanese analyse the recent past, present and possible future of their complex relationship. Together, Europeans and Japanese may still exert a major influence on the developed and the developing world.

GORDON DANIELS
Kyoto, Summer, 1985

PART I:
Europe and Japan: The Historical Setting

1
Japan in the Post-War World – Between Europe and the United States

GORDON DANIELS

Japan's surrender in August 1945 marked far more than a military catastrophe. Her defeat effectively destroyed all the diplomatic paths which she had followed in the previous century. In a world of nuclear weapons and economic interdependence a return to virtual isolation was impossible.[1] With her armed forces destroyed a revival of the independent diplomacy of the early Meiji period would have been hazardous.[2] Wartime campaigns against the British Commonwealth had made a new Anglo-Japanese alliance inconceivable, while the defeat and occupation of Germany and Italy excluded the possibility of a new Tripartite Pact.[3] Furthermore, ill-will in Japan's erstwhile empire: Taiwan, Korea, Manchuria, China and much of South East Asia, made close links with such countries a very distant prospect.[4]

This combination of forces created a painful international environment, and an American army of occupation ensured that all Japanese embassies and consulates overseas were temporarily closed. Four years after Japan's surrender the Communist revolution in China further delayed the prospect of Tokyo returning easily to her pre-war exchange of manufactures for raw materials from the Asian mainland.

Hemmed in by these circumstances it was almost inevitable that Tokyo would base its post-war foreign policy on the closest of relations with her ex-enemy, the United States. In *The White House Years* Henry Kissinger wrote 'It is odd that two such different nations should have come together' but the forces impelling Tokyo and Washington into mutual cooperation were immensely powerful.[5]

The presence of an American army of occupation, for six-and-a-half years, was a vital factor in shaping Japanese attitudes. But Japan's new outlook was far more than a simple response to military force. By the standards of much international behaviour America's occupation policies were benign and well meaning. Furthermore, by 1948, the United States had begun to convert the relationship of conqueror and conquered into a subtler and more complex alignment. American military leaders stood to gain much from links with Japanese intelligence experts who had specialised in the study of Soviet affairs. Japan provided invaluable bases in the Far East. American businessmen and congressional leaders believed that the resurgence of the Japanese economy would benefit both trans-Pacific trade and American profits.[5]

They also held that a prosperous Japan would be a stable anti-Communist partner.

Finally, there still existed a surprising number of American diplomats, missionaries, traders and scholars with deep experience of Japan who were committed to a process of intellectual and social healing – these official and unofficial envoys sought to rebuild the relations which had linked significant groups of Americans and Japanese in the years before the Pacific War. For Japanese cabinets fear of Communism, recognition of America's economic power, and hostility to rapid re-armament all helped to produce partnership with Washington and dependence upon American forces (in bases in Japan) for defence against Communist China and the Soviet Union.

These political, commercial, military and cultural relations, which were symbolised by the Peace and Security Treaties of September 1951, clearly brought many advantages; not only physical security but generous treatment of Japanese goods in the American market. The latter allowed Japan's economic growth to continue long after the Korean war boom had come to an end. Indeed, by the 1970s the United States provided a market for almost one third of Japan's increasingly sophisticated exports.

Yet the history of the new alliance was not a Utopian chronicle. Its clear inequalities of power, status and behaviour riled many in a nation whose modern history had been proud and independent. The association of the Japan-United States alliance with the struggles of the cold war often appeared dangerous; while the inherent contradiction between Japan's history and geography, which were Asiatic, and her political economy – which was dominated by North America – created deep unease in many Japanese minds. America's effective veto on formal diplomatic relations with China was also humiliating and appeared to prevent the development of what was, somewhat romantically, viewed as a vast potential market.

There were also emotive incidents which stirred anti-American feelings. Visits, of nuclear-powered warships to Japanese harbours and the suspicion that they might be carrying nuclear weapons, from time to time disturbed Japanese who recalled Hiroshima and Nagasaki. American rule in the Ryūkyū islands was at times characterised by a colonial atmosphere, and insensitivity to the wishes of local inhabitants.

But perhaps the most disturbing element in Japanese-American relations was the role of the United States in the Vietnam war. Japan's conservative leaders stood politically, if not militarily, beside America in her hostility to the Hanoi regime, but the majority of Japanese people were disturbed by the human agony inflicted by American forces on fellow Asians. Not only was the Vietnam war deeply embarrassing, but it coincided with a period of peculiar difficulty in trans-Pacific relations. Within the framework of Japanese-American cooperation the United States did make continuous concessions to Japanese demands for public recognition of a more equal relationship. In 1960 and again in 1970 Washington re-negotiated the Security

Treaty to improve the process of consultation between the two powers. America also agreed to return the Bonin Isles to Japanese administration and then to transfer Okinawa to Japan's control.[6]

But by 1971 economic frictions were troubling the alliance for the first time. In 1961 and 1963 the United States had a favourable trade balance with Japan, but between 1964 and 1965 a Japanese surplus leapt from $377 million to $1901 million. Even more serious, between 1967 and 1970 Japan's favourable balance soared from $1160 million to $3963 million, and within the next year it almost doubled.

Harrassed by the Vietnam war America was increasingly exasperated by these humiliating statistics. At this time the American diplomat Alexis Johnson declared that this problem 'had more of an adverse impact on America's international financial situation than relations with any other single country in the world'.[7]

America's irritation also exposed Japan's inner divisions in a most embarrassing way. Prime Minister Satō apparently promised that Japanese textile exports – which commanded 7% of the American market – would be restrained; but it proved almost impossible to ensure that Japan's textile industry would comply with this decision.[8] In August 1971 America replied by placing a 10% surcharge on Japanese imports, and taking measures to force up the value of the yen. Japan backed down in the face of these measures and agreed to a three-year export limit in exchange for an end to the surcharge.

For Japan these events seemed to threaten the end of an era of stability. If America could not be relied on to maintain an open door, markets would have to be sought elsewhere. What was more, America's failures in Vietnam cast doubts upon her capacity to defend Japan from possible assaults from communist powers. President Nixon talked increasingly of Asians being responsible for their own defence and Henry Kissinger's secret visit to Peking, also in 1971, created a brief panic in Tokyo. For a time there was fear that, as in the Second World War, China could become America's Far Eastern partner.

However, within months Americans and Japanese had removed each others' anxieties, and the United States soon indicated that she approved of Japan beginning diplomatic and commercial relations with the communist régime in Beijing.

For Japan the process of establishing peaceful relations with the People's Republic of China was tortuous and full of subtle symbolism. But this new situation – which was a by-product of the Sino-Soviet split – offered Japan greater security and diplomatic flexibility. It also suggested that if her exports were obstructed in North America China might form a partial alternative market. In other words in 1972 Japan's policy continued to be based on the American alliance, but the United States was no longer omnipotent and her markets could not absorb rising Japanese exports indefinitely.

If the 1960s saw the gradual accumulation of Japanese diplomatic difficulties these same years also brought rapid economic growth and the beginnings of a rising Japanese interest in the third main centre of

democratic politics and economic free enterprise – Western Europe.
Like Japan Europe had ended the war devastated, politically insecure and with little prospect of economic recovery. As in Japan, American aid, protection and political encouragement generated stability and prosperity.[9] Yet these similarities hardly implied any close links between these two beneficiaries of America's anti-Soviet stance. For some time European powers were primarily concerned with their own reconstruction and in continental Europe the tradition of close personal and political relations with Japan was far weaker than in the United States.[10]

As a result of geography, and French, British, Belgian and Dutch concern with colonial problems, interest in Japan developed slowly. What was more, anti-Japanese feeling, particularly in the Netherlands, was more persistent in Europe than in the United States. Both Western Europe and Japan were economically much weaker than Washington and were mutually suspicious in commercial matters. Japan applied to join the GATT in 1952 but after considerable resistance she was only allowed to accede to the treaty in 1955.

But this was a limited as well as a late act of acceptance. Fourteen countries including Britain, France, Belgium and the Netherlands rejected full GATT relations and invoked article 35 which provided for non-application of the agreeement between particular parties. Some twenty-seven British, French and Belgian dependencies also invoked the protection of Article 35.

Understandably, the Japanese regarded this as unjust treatment which recalled the unequal treaties dictated by European states in the nineteenth-century. Japan pressed for changes and the 1959 GATT meeting was held in Tokyo. However, Article 35 continued to be a thorn in Euro-Japanese relations and it was not until 1962 that Britain gave up this protection, as part of a broad commercial treaty.[11]

In these same years moves towards European integration came to be a matter of some concern to Japan. For the powerful United States, European unity appeared a useful aid in bolstering the non-communist camp but to Japan its implications were wholly commercial and negative. In September 1960, three years after the establishment of the European Economic Community, one commentator in Tokyo wrote:

> 'Japan has no financial stake at all inside Europe and practically no financial connections elsewhere in the world, and no spare capital to make them, even if they were economically and politically workable. And while Japan is at present a strong and active commercial economy her strength does not compare with Europe's as a bloc or with that of America. The Japanese foreign exchange reserves are currently at a peak of a million and a half dollars. This, however, is only about half that of Britain's reserves and Britain is a country only half Japan's size'.[12]

In this situation Japan feared that the creation of the EEC would lead to an introspective, narrow commercial policy in Europe, and that European economic integration would create such massive competitive power that she would suffer in third country markets. At the same time, Japanese fears were heightened by what one public relations specialist termed Europe's 'pre-war stereotyped vision of Japan as a country where low wages, market flooding tactics and political assassinations are the order of the day'.[13]

Japan was also perturbed at the prospect of the Organisation for European Economic Cooperation (OEEC) being transformed into a pan-Atlantic organisation which would exclude her from the society of industrialised powers. However, America, and later Britain, gave support to Japanese membership of the new Organisation for Economic Cooperation and Development (OECD) and by 1964 Japan had emerged as a full member of the organisation.

It is hardly surprising that Europe had a somewhat archaic image of the Japanese economy at this time for the chief items of concern – as in pre-war days – were cheap cotton textiles; domestic sewing machines were another major item of dispute. Conversely, Japan appeared alarmed that if Britain entered the EEC, this would pose a serious threat to her own emerging shipbuilding industry.

The early years of the Six saw increasingly active Japanese attempts – by ministerial visits – to improve relationships with European capitals. At this time Japan appeared as an under-privileged outsider struggling for a reasonable measure of recognition. As in later textile talks with the United States Japanese policy often suffered from inter-ministerial rivalry with the Foreign Ministry taking a more conciliatory attitude than the Ministry of International Trade and Industry (MITI).

In the mid 1960s, as in later years, Japan's Foreign Ministry (*Gaimushō*) emphasised the export of Japanese capital and productive techniques as a means of improving commercial relations. For the *Gaimushō* feared that trading friction could poison the whole atmosphere of Japan's foreign relations, thereby destroying the possibility of successful negotiations on all economic matters.

Despite all these difficulties the 1960s saw a creeping liberalisation of attitudes in both Brussels and Tokyo. In October 1969 Japan and the EEC agreed on freer trade in cotton goods and between 1960 and 1970 Japanese exports to the Six grew from $173 million to $1303 million. Imports from the EEC increased from $209 million to $1117 million and from EFTA from $157 million to $750 million.[14] As late as 1967 Japan's trade with the EEC was slightly in deficit but soon Japan's surplus was to be a dominant theme in discussions between Tokyo and Brussels.

Although Japan was beginning to succeed in Europe the significance for Japan of their mutual trade was still greatly overshadowed by trade across the Pacific. Yet this remained a time of optimism and economic growth in Europe, and attitudes towards Japan began to mellow. As Japanese products became more sophisticated the notion of Japan as a country of ill-paid primitives was increasingly discounted. As a result, by 1970 the European Parliament was calling for a broader political and economic relationship with Tokyo.

Unfortunately, optimism and very high growth rates were soon to disappear. The Middle East War of 1973 and the development of oil diplomacy by the Arab States not only drove up the price of oil but deeply affected relations between Japan and the United States. The Middle East was a crucial source of Japan's energy and when the Arab States threatened to cut off Tokyo's supplies America was manifestly unable to help – either politically or economically.

In November 1973, Japan bowed to Arab pressure and stated that she would reconsider her policy towards Israel, unless the latter withdrew from the Arab territory which she had occupied during the 1967 Middle East War. Like the failures of United States policy in Vietnam, the Middle East crisis raised further doubts in Japanese minds regarding the American alliance; or comprehensive American protection.

Just as Japan had entered European diplomacy in the 1960s, so she was compelled to enter Middle Eastern diplomacy in the 1970s. In fact the pursuit and securing of resources led Japanese foreign policy well beyond the triangle of her links with the United States and the enlarged European Communities. Latin America, Australia and South-East Asia were all seen as regions of growing economic importance.

In 1973, the rising value of the yen which was largely the result of American measures limited the rise in Japan's trade surplus with the United States. But within three years Japan's surplus was again rising rapidly, and bickering over trade became an important sub-theme in the relations of the alliance. In some respects these arguments resembled conflicts which were to arise with European competitors. America explained her declining trade performance by drawing attention to Japanese import restrictions, particularly on agricultural products, such as citrus fruit. But Japan like Europe was endowed with strong and vociferous farmers organisations which made substantial concessions very difficult. Japan eventually eased some restrictions.

Then the United States moved its criticism to other barriers – to the import of computers, and to the right of American companies to tender for contracts for Japanese state and public organisations. Many of these arguments were merely symbolic and political. For Japanese concessions, even if made, were unlikely to produce a substantial shift in Japan's surplus. On the Japanese side policy was often hard to formulate as divisions between the Foreign Ministry – which emphasised the overall welfare of the alliance – and MITI – which was more concerned with economic criteria – often blurred Japan's position.

These economic frictions and the increase in Japan's surplus had further effects on the delicate web of relations between Tokyo and Washington. Washington's frustration at Japan's economic strength led to American pressure on Japan to ease America's military burden in the Far East by increasing her land, sea and air forces. Washington also hoped that Japanese purchases of technically advanced American military aircraft would help to shift the trade balance a few degrees in America's favour. Japan was reluctant to move rapidly in this direction. Throughout much of the 1970s rapid and substantial rearmament was unpopular in Japan and at times there was fear that such moves might irritate Japan's immediate neighbours.

If defence was one area of continuing if polite friction between Japan and the United States another more sensitive issue was unemployment in sectors of the American economy stemming from Japanese imports. Japan's technical effectiveness in manufacturing and marketing small cars coincided with the rising price of petrol and led to massive sales of compact cars which had previously been thought unsuitable for the American market.

Increasingly, American manufacturers pressed for restrictions on Japanese exports. But there were also more enlightened suggestions that Japanese companies should build factories in the United States to relieve unemployment and soften the demand for protection. Yet any substantial Japanese response to these proposals was scarcely within the power of diplomats; it was much more dependent upon the decisions of private companies, and such developments were slow to gain momentum. Indeed, under the Reagan administration temporary agreements on 'voluntary restraints' proved the main palliative in this field.

Despite these frictions between the Pacific partners, Japan has remained committed to the alliance and has sought to support its military fabric as far as possible. President Carter's suggestion that United States forces might be withdrawn from South Korea stimulated active Japanese resistance. This contributed significantly to reversing American policy.

Japan's sense of danger – that the East Asian military balance might be upset – seemed further justified by Russian behaviour in the disputed northern islands between Hokkaido and the Kurile chain.[15] In 1979 and 1980 Soviet forces on these remote territories were significantly increased and the discovery of a Soviet spy ring in the Japanese self-defence forces produced further alarm. This Japanese unease was also augmented by the Soviet invasion of Afghanistan, the Vietnamese conquest of Cambodia and increasingly close relations between Moscow and Hanoi. These events all changed Japanese views of defence and world politics in the early 1980s.

In her search for markets and raw materials Japan had long pursued a so-called 'multi-directional' diplomacy. Now Tokyo turned to a clearer and more overt commitment to links with the United States and the non-communist world. It may be argued that Japan's improved relations with mainland China, since 1972, have improved her military position, but what Japan sees as Soviet expansionism seems a particularly serious danger. This sense of threat has not only been voiced by American and Japanese political leaders – Prime Minister Ohira's Investigation Group into Comprehensive National Security, which reported in July 1980 clearly stated:

'The military nature of the Soviet Union's foreign relations is becoming increasingly obvious. This was confirmed decisively by the Soviet intervention in Afghanistan. Soviet diplomacy strongly reflects the philosophy of power.[16]

Even more striking has been the increasing feeling among the Japanese public, encouraged by the Japanese Government, that the Soviet Union's military strength in the Far East demands an increase in Japan's defence forces. This has brought no dramatic changes, but the purchase of anti-submarine ships and aircraft, increases in the defence budget, and the weakening of popular hostility to the self-defence forces have all been significant developments.[17]

Japan's military and non-military policies have not only become more clearly directed to the support of United States policy, but her use of economic aid to strengthen states in the front line of great power rivalry may have helped to ease American pressure for yet more defence spending.

In 1980 and after Japan has given financial aid to areas well beyond South-East Asia, the region usually considered of immediate interest to her. Such countries as Jamaica, Pakistan and Turkey have all benefitted from this new turn in Japanese policy. Repeatedly, whether the issue has been the Middle East, Indo-China, Afghanistan or Poland, Japan has made overt statements opposing the Communist use of force in settling international or domestic disputes. In this respect the political dimension of the alliance with the United States has come to be more public, as America's military protection has seemed increasingly important.

Geography, military power and the absence of an historical relationship have prevented Japan's post-war relations with Western Europe paralleling those with the United States or South East Asia. But in the last decade Tokyo's relations with Brussels have been transformed. Not only have memories of wartime Japan ceased to exert a significant influence on Europeans minds, but in informal ways – such as the activities of the Trilateral Commission – and formal negotiations, the notion of a triangular partnership has gained increasing strength.

At a time when communist and third world powers pursue varieties of authoritarian and protectionist policies, Japan, America and Western Europe are increasingly seen as angles of a triangle which are essential to the survival of a liberal political and economic order.

The new importance which Japan has placed upon economic relations with Europe has been symbolised by the establishment, in 1975, of the Japanese diplomatic mission to the European Communities. There have also been frequent exchanges of visits by powerful commercial and industrial delegations and an increasing number of regular high-level consultations. Yet these exchanges have been far from harmonious.

Like Britain in its nineteenth-century heyday, Japan has strenuously opposed restrictions on her industrial exports. This has often brought conflict with leaders in Western Europe. But in pursuing this policy Japan has often been helped by the uncertain nature of the European Community as a political unit. Given Japan's general consensus on commercial policy, it is hardly surprising that the Community failed, in 1972, in its attempt to negotiate an overall commercial treaty with Japan which would provide safeguards in the event of a sudden inrush of Japanese products. At that time Japan successfully argued that the GATT already provided such safeguards and that no further measures were necessary. Yet despite such clashes and European condemnation of Japanese 'non-tariff barriers' this failure to agree on a treaty produced no permanent disruption of Euro-Japanese relations.

In fact Japan has constantly sought to soften European criticism of her export strategy by a number of direct and indirect measures. She has arranged for European businessmen to have marketing conferences in Japan. She has lowered a number of tariffs in a series of liberalising measures and has agreed to 'voluntary' export restraints on sensitive products. Japanese diplomats have also pointed out the inaccuracy of some European claims regarding the total inpenetrability of the Japanese market.

In 1978, Japan's surplus with the EEC reached $5 billion and the Community called for substantial symbolic action to reduce it. More than once, Japan has undertaken to attempt to reduce her rising surplus – but by definition a pattern of largely free trade cannot be subject to massive manipulation. Furthermore, Japanese companies have great independent power and would resist instructions to fall in line with government plans for large purchases of European equipment. It is difficult to escape the conclusion that the troublesome trade surplus is not the result of exotic non-tariff barriers of a conspiratorial character. To a large extent it is the product of Japanese technology, efficiency and marketing which are rarely matched by European enterprises.

Attempts to view these conflicts in simplistic terms have fortunately weakened as both sides have come to recognise the complexity of the issues involved. In the 1980s both Japanese and Europeans have suggested ameliorating problems by joint research projects, and the building of Japanese factories in Europe. Although high labour costs in such countries as West Germany have deterred Japanese investment, the number of Japanese factories in Europe has gradually increased. This trend has been particularly marked in the United Kingdom where the Thatcher Government has urged Japanese car and electronics companies to establish plants inside the European tariff wall.

Japanese policy has at times been assisted by the varied and inconsistent restrictions imposed by various Community countries and the mutual differences among European states. Furthermore, European admiration for Japanese efficiency has also encouraged the idea of industrial cooperation. More recently, American and Japanese proposals for a 'Pacific Community' have created fears that Europe might be neglected. This has also strengthened moves in Europe towards improved relations with Japanese Government and industry. As a result, Japan has clearly moved from a position of some political and economic inferiority to a position of equality and self-confidence.

Increasingly, Japanese economic successes are understood rather than denigrated in Europe and the broad interdependence of Europe and Japan is recognised by both parties. Japan's trade has been aided by the European Community's many internal divisions but its success has been overwhelmingly the result of her entrepreneurs' triumphs in the very contest-free competition, which is said to epitomise transactions in the Euro-Japanese-American triangle.

It might be argued that the present situation is economically satisfactory for Japan, but if Japan's position is too be more secure, understanding of Japanese commerce and politics needs to be far more widespread in European society. Conversely, the Japanese might question whether, in a dangerous world, existing economic relations are sufficient to sustain friendship between Japan and Western Europe.

It would be platitudinous to claim that personal contacts can resolve such serious problems as unemployment, but even today the formal and informal associations of politicians, businessmen and scholars which characterise trans-Pacific relations do not exist in relations between Europe and Japan. For Japan it is most important that she be more widely understood in Europe. But it is also important that Japan should view Europe with more interest and sympathy. That the Japanese Society for the Study of the European Communities published its first yearbook as late as 1981 suggests a somewhat tardy beginning.[18]

When one recalls the programme of Fulbright scholarships which did much to promote understanding of the United States after the Second World War one can only conclude that Japan still has much to gain from a more energetic cultural policy towards Western Europe. On repeated occasions officials of the Japan Foundation have asserted the paramount importance of South-East Asia and America, and despite some improvements it is still doubtful if Europe receives adequate attention.[19]

In the years since the Second World War Japan's multi-level partnership with the United States has survived commercial, emotional, political and cultural challenges. Its origins were dictated by cruel circumstance but it has outlasted the Anglo-Japanese Alliance which was a voluntary agreement. Now the American-Japanese alliance as embodied by President Reagan and Premier Nakasone is so mature that it resembles the partnerships which binds the élites of English-speaking or West European states.

However, relations between Japan and Europe are very different. At their base they lack the hard military foundation of the Japanese-American alliance. At the higher levels of intellect or in the forum of public opinion there remains a need for closer relations, more information and greater informality. For relations between Japan and Europe to be secure, they require supra-commercial and suprapolitical dimensions. Without such enrichment the liberal triangle will remain an ineffective vision rather than a creative reality.

NOTES

1. Japan's foreign relations were limited to restricted contacts with China, the Netherlands and Korea from the early seventeenth-century until 1854.
2. Japan carried out a vigorous independent diplomacy from the Meiji Restoration (1868) until the signature of the Anglo-Japanese Alliance in 1902.
3. Japan signed the Tripartite Pact with Germany and Italy in September 1940.
4. For example, diplomatic relations with South Korea were not established until 1965.
5. Henry Kissinger, *The White House Years* (Boston, Mass, Little Brown, 1979) p.322.
6. The agreement to return the Bonin Islands was signed in April 1967, that to return the Ryūkyūs, including Okinawa in June 1971.
7. Frank C. Langdon, *Japan's Foreign Policy* (Vancouver, University of British Columbia Press, 1973) pp.150-151.
8. For the complexities of these negotiations see Kissinger, *The White House Years*, pp.329-340.
9. For a recent study of American-European cooperation after the Second World War see R.J. Barnet, *The Allies; America-Europe-Japan Makers of the Postwar World* (New York, Simon and Shuster, 1983).
10. American military power excluded European states such as Britain, France and the Netherlands from any meaningful role in the Occupation of Japan (1945-52) see Roger Buckley, *Occupation Diplomacy* (Cambridge, Cambridge University Press, 1982).
11. For a survey of early post-war relations between Japan and Europe see Masamichi Hanabusa, *Trade Problems Between Japan and Western Europe* (Farnborough, Hants, Gower R.I.I.A. 1979) pp.1-15.
12. Joseph Z. Reday, 'Japan Will Have to Face Common Market Troubles', *Japan Times*, 23 September 1960.
13. Charles E. Allen of Hill and Knowland Inc. reported in the *Japan Times*, 9 December 1960. Significantly, this was written shortly after the *only* post-war assassination of a major political leader – that of the Socialist, Asanuma, on 12 October 1960.
14. EFTA – The European Free Trade Association, of which the United Kingdom was a member before joining the EEC, in 1973.
15. For surveys of Soviet military activities in areas close to Japan see the Defense Agency's annual *Defense of Japan* (Tokyo) and the Research Institute for Peace and Security's (Tokyo) annual *Asian Security*.
16. The Comprehensive National Security Study Group, *Report on Comprehensive National Security* (Translation), 2 July 1980, p.52.
17. In late 1984 a Prime Ministerial advisory group recommended the abandonment of the 1 per cent of GNP limit on defence spending. This indicated a considerable shift in Japan's political mood.
18. *Nihon-EC Gakkai Nempō* (1981). Later issues appeared in 1982, 1983 and 1984. All were published by Yūhikaku, Tokyo.
19. In 1981 Asia absorbed 34% of the Foundation's overseas spending, North America 15% and Europe 19%, Kokusai Kōryū Kikin, *Kokusai Kōryū Kikin Nenpō, 57 Nendo* (Tokyo, 1982), p.46.

2
Political Development, Decision-Making and Foreign Policy in Modern Japan

ISHIDA TAKESHI

Foreign policy decisions in modern Japan are made within a structure which displays elements of continuity and change. After 1945 the aggressive, expansionist policies of pre-war days suddenly gave way to passive, reactive attitudes. Despite this stark surface contrast there remains an underlying element of continuity in Japan's foreign policy-making process. This can be traced in a fundamental way, to its relation to the overall pattern of Japan's political development.

If we define political development as *increasing governmental efficiency in utilising the human and material resources of the nation for national goals*,[1] then Japan's case must, presumably, be one of the most successful. Such a definition, however, neglects the crucial issue of the origin of national goals; how they are formulated, and by whom. Prior to 1945 Japan's national goal was to increase her national wealth and military power so as to compete with the major western states. This goal appeared to be supported by a national consensus, but it was not the product of a democratic process of decision-making.

Once the goal had been formulated by the ruling élite it was pursued effectively, but with utter disregard for the welfare of the Japanese people or of the inhabitants of areas abroad which were targets of invasion. It is axiomatic that an undemocratic decision-making process imposes few restraints upon a state which is acting in the name of presumed national goals. In fact, it was lack of sensitivity to the crucial qualitative importance of the decision-making process, which contributed significantly to the catastrophic course of Japanese political development towards war and defeat.

Here, one historical example may be cited illustrating the fact that in modern Japan policy *execution* by the bureaucracy was efficient, whereas the policy decision-making process was not considered so important. This feature of Japanese politics became increasingly evident as the Japanese pattern of modernisation developed.

The example is the clear contrast between the attitudes of Japanese political leaders towards the Russo-Japanese War (1904-1905) and the Second World War. In the former conflict, and from its beginning, political leaders seriously considered how to terminate the war. But during the Second World War when the Minister for Greater East Asia, Aoki Kazuo, was questioned in the Diet about post-war planning he reprimanded the questioner, saying 'While the nation is making all efforts to win the war, it is not appropriate to talk about the post-war situation'. The modern Japanese political system was successful in reproducing able bureaucrats, but not political leaders with a deep sense of responsibility for decision-making.

As a result of Japan's defeat in 1945 the national goal of increased wealth and military power was abandoned. Indeed the reaction against ultranationalism was so widespread that no new national goal was formulated. In a negative sense, the pursuit of military power was explicitly repudiated as a goal by the 'Peace Constitution' of 1946, which renounced war. However, since that time there has been a tacit consensus to strive for a higher GNP.

Although post-war reforms introduced parliamentary democracy, and formally liberalised the political decision-making process, the process has not been used to formulate any new, explicit national objectives. As neglect of the importance of decision-making has persisted, and the tacit consensus for a higher GNP has never been clearly formulated in the democratic process, adequate examination of this goal's suitability has also been lacking. It is only problems, such as pollution, which have resulted from rapid economic growth, which have compelled citizens to re-examine this type of economic development which is based on tacit consensus.

Bearing in mind these general characteristics of Japanese political development it is appropriate to examine decision-making in foreign policy. Here, too, lack of sensitivity to the importance of decision-making is a basic characteristic. This should not be taken to mean that there is any lack of interest in differences of opinion, or in the process of coordinating different opinions. On the contrary, Japanese political leaders are often so intent upon mediating conflicting views and creating a harmonious consensus that they avoid making decisions which might provoke controversy. In reality, of course a harmonious consensus can rarely be expected. Therefore this tendency often results in wait-and-see policies or *ad hoc* remedies for real problems – instead of mature policy decisions. Such passive attitudes towards processes of change are equally noticeable in both foreign and domestic policy.

When the question of cementing Japan's anti-communist pact with Nazi Germany and Fascist Italy was raised in the late 1930s attempts to coordinate the varying opinions of political leaders made little progress. Even though the army wanted to establish a closer alliance with Nazi Germany more than seventy meetings among government ministers could not produce any concrete decision.

The announcement of the Nazi-Soviet non-aggression pact (August 1939) then obviated the plan and also caused the collapse of the Hiranuma cabinet. Thereafter, a strengthened alliance only became possible after Japanese leaders considered that German hegemony in Europe was assured. In internal politics, too, the *fait accompli* of the military forced political leaders to conceal divisions of opinion. Army officers stationed in China in the 1930s often engaged in military adventures without the consent of the central government, while the latter sought to remedy the effects of such incidents, rather than impose its control.

Studies of the historical process of Japan's aggression in China have clearly disproved the hypotheses of some writers, that Japan's leaders were acting on the basis of a secret plan from the very beginning. In fact, there are many scholars who have pointed to similarities between Japan's invasion of China and the Vietnam war, in the sense that both Japan and the United States gradually committed themselves to hostilities by successive administrative actions.

There was no explicit political decision to declare war. There is, however, one marked difference between the two conflicts. Whereas Japan was unable to terminate her war before she suffered defeat, there were domestic elements in the United States working to end the Vietnam war.

There is one valuable example which illustrates the importance of 'established facts' in modern Japan. In 1931 one of the planners of Japan's expansion in Manchuria, Lieutenant Colonel Ishihara Kanji wrote:

> 'Theoretically it is rational first to carry out the necessary domestic reforms so as to be prepared for a total war, but in reality this is so difficult that it is more practical to commence hostilities first, as an established fact. Once the war is begun, with victories, public opinion will follow, and the reform of domestic politics for a total war becomes easier'.[2]

Although Ishihara later lost his influence in the army, this tactic of creating 'established facts' became the main means for the army to achieve its ends. The lack of a regular decision-making process and the accumulation of 'established facts' often forced the central government to acquiesce in strategies convenient to the army.

This Japanese lack of decision-making could be related to the structure which Professor Hosoya Chihiro terms a truncated pyramid system without integrated leadership at the top.[3] In institutional terms this system was rooted in the weak position of the prime minister as a *primus inter pares* who was not empowered to dismiss ministers. It was also related to the privileged position of the army and navy, which were viewed as directly subordinate to the Emperor in the pre-war period.

The difficulties of decision-making in a truncated pyramid system are exemplified in various historical cases. For instance, Theo Sommer's study of German-Japanese diplomatic relations from 1935 to 1940, contrasts Nazi Germany, in which policy was clearly decided by the *Führer*, with militarist Japan in which policy did not flow from any single decision-making process.[4] Also in terms of ideology of the anti-democratic ideological elements listed by Professor Sontheimer, all, except one were present in militarist Japan. That exception is precisely an emphasis on '*Entscheidung*' (decision).[5]

One result of post-war institutional reforms in Japan is that the Prime Minister is now empowered to dismiss ministers who disturb the 'integration' of the cabinet. In addition, the army and navy have ceased to be privileged institutions under the Emperor's command. Thus, there is no institutional hindrance to integrated decision-making. However, in terms of political culture, continuity exists in the tendency to avoid clear-cut decision-making so as to avoid fuelling serious factional conflicts within the ruling party.

In his study of Japanese foreign policy Frank Langdon pointed out that Prime Ministers Ikeda (1960-64) and Satō (1964-72) sought to minimise factional conflicts over diplomatic issues so as to maintain the coalition of supporting factions. The result was virtually no change in international policy.[6] This tendency has been a feature of almost all post-war conservative cabinets.

Another related result of factional conflicts within the ruling party is the relatively important role of opposition parties, particularly regarding foreign policy. The Kishi cabinet collapsed in 1960 when conflict with opposition parties over the US Security Treaty created fatal factional tensions within the government party. Although opposition parties have been unable to exert any positive influence upon foreign policy decisions they have been influential in that, with public support, they have been able to prevent the rapid rearmament demanded by the United States and desired by the Japanese right wing. Criticism from opposition parties has triggered factional conflicts within the ruling party and has been an important obstacle to a rapid increase in military commitment to the United States.

Japan's democratic system of decision-making has created leeway for various interest groups to exert pressure, and has made decision-making processes more complicated and protracted. When various interests play the role of vetoing groups – aiming in opposing directions – preservation of the status quo, or 'wait and see' becomes the preferred policy. In particular, at election time, candidates are anxious to appeal to mutually related interest groups to secure block votes. For example, this explains why the liberalisation of the import of grapefruit and other commodities was delayed for more than a year – until the 1972 election was over. Sometimes conflict between ministries which have close links with differing interest groups also increases 'pluralistic stagnation' in foreign policy-making.

It is an historical irony that one result of the democratisation of the Japanese political process has been 'pluralistic stagnation' and hence the continuation of a lack of integrated decision-making. In pre-war and war-time Japan such privileged elements as senior statesmen, and in exceptional cases, the Emperor, fulfilled an important function in overcoming the defects of the 'truncated pyramid system'. But in the post-war period such mechanisms no longer exist.

Because of the absence of such mechanisms, and of critical decisions of war and peace, genuine cases of decision-taking in foreign policy have been rare in the post-war years. One such case concerned the reopening of diplomatic relations with the Soviet Union in 1956. At that time, Prime Minister Hatoyama's undertaking to retire after resolving this issue reduced factional strife within the government party.[7] Another important case of decision-making in foreign policy was the normalisation of diplomatic relations with the People's Republic of China, beginning with Prime Minister Tanaka's visit to Beijing in 1972. This reflected strong leadership on the part of Prime Minister Tanaka, but it was also an *ad hoc* reponse to America's sudden rapprochement with China in 1971-72, the first of the Nixon 'shocks'.

Traditional political culture in Japan preferred the cultivation of consensus, rather than clear-cut decision-making. This tendency was related to a strong emphasis on personal relations in politics; in the sense that consensus was expected to develop naturally out of close personal relationships. There are several historical examples which illustrate this attitude. Immediately before the outbreak of war with the United States the Prime Minister, Prince Konoe, was convinced that a personal talk with President Roosevelt would, if it could be arranged, be sufficient to prevent war.

Yoshida Shigeru, Japan's ambassador in London from 1936 to 1938, tried unsuccessfully, to make advantageous use of his personal contacts with British political leaders. Later, however, when he became a post-war Prime Minister his personal contact with General MacArthur proved invaluable, avoiding many routine negotiations with the occupation bureaucracy.

With one exception Yoshida's successors were not career diplomats; nor did they boast sufficient command of English to cultivate personal contacts. Also, they had not previously encountered authoritarian leaders such as Douglas MacArthur. Later, at summit conferences, no Japanese Prime Minister had sufficient linguistic skill to carry on talks without the help of interpreters. They remained silent or vague in expressing views about Japan's international role. The problem was not only one of foreign language aptitude, but of lack of clear ideas about Japan's international position. West Germany, which like Japan was defeated in the Second World War rejoined the international community, in the form of the United Nations, much later than Japan; but she has played a far more prominent role than Japan in East-West relations, particularly after the introduction of Willy Brandt's '*Ostpolitik*'.

Of course, one must take account of the different international positions of Japan and Germany in the post-war world. At least until the 1960s Japan was subject to the overwhelming influence of American foreign policy. Under the American Occupation (1945-52) Japan had no normal diplomatic relations. Thereafter her foreign policy was dominated by American ties. In contrast, Germany was in the centre of Europe, politically divided, and involved in more complex relationships.

During this period, therefore, Japanese leaders lacked adequate opportunities of practical training in diplomatic decision-making. It was not until after the 1973 oil crisis, and trade conflicts with the

United States that Japanese political leaders confronted a serious need for foreign policy decisions independent of those of the United States. More specifically, Japan's relationship with Europe has never attracted sufficient attention in post-war foreign policy. This is chiefly the legacy of Japan's dependence on the United States during the Occupation period.

Much the same can be said about Japan's relations with Third World countries. In the post-war years Japan took particular interest in the South-East Asian territories which she had occupied during the Second World War, because of reparations problems and the need to normalise diplomatic relations. But it was only the oil crisis of 1973 which forced Japan's leaders to be aware of the importance of relations with oil producing states in the Middle East and developing countries elsewhere.

In comparison with the United States and South-East Asia, European countries have been of lesser importance in the eyes of post-war Japanese leaders. If one recalls the importance of the Anglo-Japanese Alliance in the early twentieth century and the attention Japan paid to Europe prior to 1945 this change is quite remarkable.

Even after the Second World War Japanese intellectuals continued to have a deeper interest in Europe than the mass of Japanese people. Many thought that some European countries provided the model for a welfare state. When Japanese were asked where they would prefer to live if they were to reside abroad those of higher educational background usually tended to prefer Europe to the United States.

This intellectual interest in Europe declined when many began to think that European economies had performed poorly in the aftermath of the oil crisis. Only recently have trade frictions between Japan and Europe forced Japanese leaders to pay greater attention to Europe than before. Even so, trade problems with the United States still overshadow difficulties with Europe. Thus, the general immobilism in Japanese foreign policy has created even more serious difficulties in economic and political relations with Europe.

It may be claimed that Japan's lack of strong foreign policy, leadership and decision-making in the post-war years has been advantageous. Many risks have been successfully avoided. Some benefits are undeniable, but only in conditions where there is no independent political force capable of imposing *faits accomplis* on the government. So long as the military forces which exist under the 'Peace Constitution' remain subordinate to the democratic process; and so long as international pressures, for example American demands for greater military commitments, are not so intense as to irritate Japan, then lack of strong leadership may be harmless. However, under changed conditions the pre-war pattern of passively administering 'established facts' might recur – with catastrophic results.

Since Japan is currently considered to be an 'economic superpower' her potential international role is the focus of great attention. As a result, even Japanese non-action will have important consequences. If Japan's aid to the Third World is insufficient this will provoke criticism. If a *laissez-faire* policy regarding exports disturbs international markets there will be criticism from trading partners. In view of this situation Japan cannot afford to maintain its 'truncated pyramid' system of leadership – whatever advantages it may have afforded in the past.

NOTES

1. A.F.K. Organski, *The Stages of Political Development*, New York, Alfred Knopf, 1965, p.7 (Italics in the original).
2. Ishihara Kanji, 'Manmō Mondai Shiken' in Tsunoda Jun (ed) *Ishihara Kanji Shiryō:Kokubōronsaku*, Tokyo, Hara Shobō, 1971, p.78.
3. Hosoya Chihiro, *Nihon Gaikō no Zahyō*,Tokyo, Chūōkōronsha, 1979, p.207.
4. Theo Sommer, *Deutschland und Japan zwischen Mächten, 1935-1940*, Tübingen, Mohr, 1962. There was a duality of diplomacy in Germany between the Ministry of Foreign Affairs and Ribbentrop's office, until Ribbentrop became Minister of Foreign Affairs in February 1983.
5. Kurt Sontheimer, *Antidemokratisches Denken in der Weimarer Republik*, Munich, Nymphenburger Verlagshandlung, 1968.
6. Frank C. Langdon, *Japan's Foreign Policy*, Vancouver, B.C. University of British Columbia Press, 1973, Chapter 9.
7. Donald C. Hellman, *Japanese Foreign Policy and Domestic Politics*, Berkeley and Los Angeles, University of California Press, 1969.

PART II:
Euro-Japanese Relations: The Contemporary Scene

3
The Economic and Non-Economic Dimensions of Euro-Japanese Relations

ENDYMION WILKINSON*

1. INTRODUCTION

One hundred years ago three-quarters of world industrial capacity was situated in North-West Europe and on the Atlantic seaboard of the United States. Since then industrialisation has spread both westwards and eastwards to East Asia. Today, as a consequence, the world is divided into four major industrial regions. In order of size these are (1) the Americas and (2) Western Europe, each of which roughly accounts for 20-25% of world industrial output: (3) the Soviet Union and its satellites, and (4) Japan and the East Asian industrialising countries, each of which roughly accounts for between 15-20% of world industrial capacity.

A striking feature of these shares of world product is that between 1960 and 1980, the Western European and North American shares both declined by four per cent, the share of the USSR and its satellites declined by two per cent, while the share of Japan and the East Asian region increased by seven per cent. (Over the same period OPEC gained a mere two percentage points moving from three per cent of world product in 1960 to five per cent in 1980).

Prior to and accompanying these changes in the world balance of economic power has been a weakening of Europe's political influence in the world including its influence on Japan. The current weakness of Europe's relations with Japan can be shown in the simple diagram overleaf which sums up the relations between Europe, Japan and the USA.

While Japan and Europe both have cultural, political, security and economic interests linking them with the USA and the USA with them, the weak side of the triangle is the Japan-Europe side. Not only are there no direct security links, but the political links until recently have been tenuous. Above all, Europe's 'economic impulse' towards

---

*Dr Wilkinson is currently the Deputy Head of the Delegation of the Commission of the European Communities for South-East Asia. The views expressed in this Chapter are his own and do not necessarily reflect those of the EC Commission. For a fuller discussion of the ideas presented here, see the author's Japan versus Europe, a History of Misunderstanding, revised edition, Penguin Books, London, 1983.

Asia and Japan has grown far weaker (see dotted arrow) than Japan's 'economic impulse' towards Europe and its neighbouring regions. Likewise, Europe's cultural influence over Japan is today greatly diminished.

This is in direct contrast to the situation one hundred years ago when Europe was clearly much more powerful than Japan. Then it seemed only natural for the Europeans to teach and for the Japanese to learn. Today, the roles are reversed. Now European involvement in Asia, especially during the nineteenth-century, appears merely a temporary intervention in the full sweep of Asian history. In many ways, the situation today has reverted to pre-nineteenth-century patterns. China is again united, Japan is vastly strengthened and the European presence in Asia is once more marginal.

In line with these changes it is only natural that European trade with East Asia is less important today than it was in the last century. Indeed, in several cases, including Japan, there has been a reversion to the old pattern of the European trade as a luxury trade. The difference is that now, Japan is an increasingly serious trade rival, not only in third markets in Asia, but also in the United States and in markets throughout the world, including Europe's backyard and Europe itself.

One hundred years ago it was the Japanese who complained of sudden influxes of European goods disrupting domestic industries. Today, the boot is on the other foot and it is the turn of Europeans and Americans to plead with the Japanese to restrain their exports.

The roles have been reversed in other spheres too. In the nineteenth-century, Europeans regarded Japan as an exotic playground, the ultimate in sophisticated tourism, while the Japanese regarded Europe as a disciplined, group-oriented society possessing the secrets of efficient industrial production. Today, it is the Japanese who flock to Europe for exotic tourism and it is the Europeans who increasingly regard Japan as a disciplined society with amazingly efficient industries.

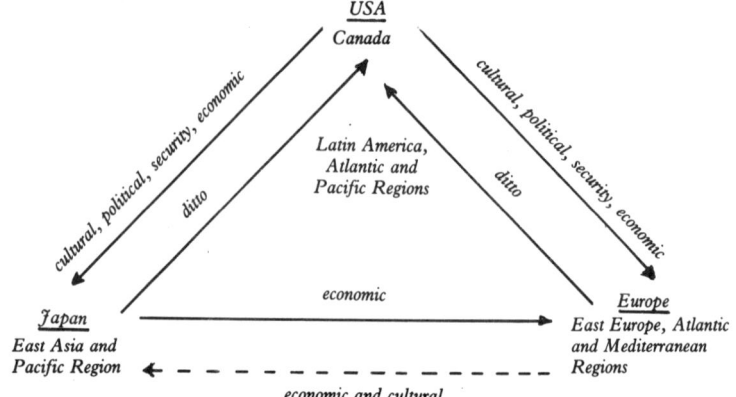

Relations between Europe, Japan and the USA, including spheres closest to them

If the withdrawal of Europe from East Asia has inevitably meant that direct political and security relations with Japan are fewer today than in the past, the rise of Japan as one of the world's largest economic powers has introduced new forms of interaction with Europe.

Firstly, these are indirect and concerned with multilateral economic issues rather than with geopolitics. Europe and Japan share many common values, they also face many of the same problems: the need to maintain their independence in a world of superpowers; the need for access to raw materials and energy supplies as well as access to export markets. In seeking solutions to these problems they are objective allies. They have a shared interest in maintaining an open trading system even if they compete strongly within that system.

Secondly, just at a time when European political interests have moved away from Asia, Japan's increasingly large role in the world economy has meant that her interests have moved closer to Europe and to the Mediterranean region. This shift in spheres of action marks a fundamental change in the world balance of economic power. It has also been the principal cause of friction, mainly of an economic and commercial nature, in the bilateral relations between Japan and Europe.

These long-run changes in the economic and political roles of Europe and Japan in the world have not yet been accompanied by a corresponding adjustment of either Europe or Japan's views of each other. Old images have persisted, thereby impeding communication and exacerbating trade frictions.

Trade frictions have usually occurred when a decline in domestic demand in Japan, leading to strong pressures to export, coincides with a downturn of the business cycle in Europe, especially in labour-intensive industries. Reflecting Japan's previous negative balance of payments, the yen at such times tends to be undervalued, thus giving Japan's exports an added advantage.

The knife has been given a further twist when in addition to scoring surpluses in trade with Europe, the Japanese balance of payments moves into the black while her partners remain in the red. This happened during the Great Depression of 1929-32 and again during the 1970s and early 1980s when massive rises in the price of oil and other raw materials created a sharp new stimulus for Japan to export. Indeed the oil shocks of 1973 and 1979 triggered huge Japanese export booms which led directly to trade frictions with both Europe and America.

There are of course many other reasons why trade frictions have broken out between Japan and Europe. One conditioning factor is that both partners are poor in natural resources so that their trade is almost entirely in industrial goods. This is in striking contrast to Japan's trade with other major regions of the world; North and South America, Australasia, the Middle East, China and South-East Asia – all of which include raw materials as an important element of their exports to Japan. The result is that the pattern of their trade with her is far more complementary than Europe's. Today Europe and Japan are in direct competition with each other.

Furthermore, the nature of their competition has changed very rapidly: in the early days Japan's advantage in industries such as textiles lay in cheap labour. Competition was primarily price competition. More recently, however, as Japan has developed her capital-intensive and knowledge-intensive industries, her comparative advantage has been in technology and efficiency, not in cheap labour. So competition today is less in price than in quality. In one sense, then, the trade frictions can be seen as resulting from the growing technology gap between Europe and Japan.

The reaction in Europe to the latest Japanese challenge was often inadequate, geared more to the previous age when cheap exports from Japan were the problem. Insufficient efforts were made to meet the challenge by restructuring industries and by adopting new technologies.

A positive reaction was made even more difficult by the fact that Japan's export drives, which built up very swiftly, were often concentrated in precisely those European industries which were, for various reasons, already in decline. Moreover, these industries included some of the largest in the entire economy – steel, shipbuilding, cars, bearings and electronics. The very core of the industrial economy seemed threatened and political lobbies were quickly aroused.

Japan was accused of operating with all kinds of unfair advantages, of keeping her own markets closed and of exporting unemployment.

The most recent Japanese export drives have also come at a time when the principal economies of the world are far more tightly interconnected than ever before, but when the expansion of world trade and economic growth have slowed down and the floating exchange rate system has been less and less effective in contributing to balance of payments adjustments. To make matters worse, in many European countries inflation, high levels of unemployment and falling productivity have become the norm.

Under these conditions timely restructuring of industries, and development of strategies to cope with the Japanese challenge, have been that much more difficult, instead there have been continual bouts of trade friction.

These frictions have both a positive and a negative aspect. On the positive side they have stimulated both Europeans and Japanese to take a clear look at each other, to overcome the indifference which had characterised their relations in much of the post-war period. On the other hand, the trade frictions risk enforcing negative stereotypes and, should they get completely out of control, they could eventually produce many unpleasant consequences including the breakdown of the international trading system.

2. TOWARDS CLOSER POLITICAL RELATIONS BETWEEN EUROPE AND JAPAN

To prevent the trade frictions getting out of hand, there are clearly actions to be taken in the economic, monetary and trade fields. But for these to be fully effective much closer political relations and much more efficient channels of communication have to be established between Europe and Japan.

In this respect it is worth reminding ourselves that Europe and Japan share many of the same political values and face many of the same economic problems. It is in their common interest, therefore, to strengthen political links and never to allow bilateral economic disputes to obscure their fundamental identity of purpose. Again, because Western Europe and Japan depend so heavily on regular supplies of oil from the Middle East, both have an enormous stake in ensuring stability in that region.

Although direct defence cooperation between Europe and Japan is far less important to both than the security ties by which each is firmly linked with the United States, there are surely areas where Europe and Japan could both benefit by increasing such cooperation which is at present almost nil. The incentives are not hard to find.

The Soviet Union is considered the main threat to both, so it matters greatly to Japan what happens in the European theatre, the primary focus of Soviet military power. Likewise Europeans recognise that instability in the Asia-Pacific region could readily affect the distribution of Soviet forces. European and American sales of arms and military equipment to China could eventually have more direct repercussions on Japan than on Europe (if only by stimulating a greater Soviet presence in East Asia), so the speed and extent of the Chinese military build-up is another important question of mutual concern. Responses to Soviet interventions in other parts of the world also require coordination, as do economic relations with the Soviet bloc and strategic aid to friendly countries such as Egypt, Turkey or Thailand.

Because Europe and Japan depend so heavily on regular supplies of oil from the Middle East, both have an enormous stake in contributing to stability in that region. Finally, the United Kingdom and France still have dependent territories in the Pacific. These are few and far between, but not without importance in an age of two-hundred mile territorial limits, and certainly not without considerable strategic value, to Japan, even more than to Europe.

Given these mutual interests and recognising the neccesity of a global approach to national and regional security, Europe and Japan have little to lose and much to gain by instituting, as a first step, regular exchanges of information on defence matters.[1]

Let us now turn to the question of Japan's contribution to the alliance linking her to the US and through the US to the other advanced industrial democracies. Without calling into question her Peace Constitution, there is surely room for Japan to contribute a little more to defence than she does at present. That she can afford to there can be no reasonable doubt. In 1981 and again in 1982, Japan's GNP amounted to 20% of the total GNP of the six most important members of the Western alliance, but her defence expenditures only came to approximately 4% of their total defence costs.

In 1982, the US spent 7.2% of its GNP on defence. The USSR spent about 15%, Britain 5.1%, Germany 4.3%, France 4.1% and even neutral Sweden and Switzerland, 3.1% and 2.1% respectively. Japan spent 1.0%. In 1982, the United States spent $938 per capita on defence; Britain $432, France $408, Germany $461, Italy $156, and neutral Sweden and Switzerland $365 and $320 respectively. Japan spent $87[2]

But before embarking on increased military expenditures, both Japan and her allies should be clear as to the nature and extent of her defence role. For a start, what are the defence requirements facing Japan? How can Japan's defence capability be improved? Should Japan continue the current strategy under the US nuclear umbrella of protecting only the islands of Japan? Or should she seek to cover her economic lifelines, such as the oil routes in South-East Asia, by increasing her naval and air strength? Finally, should she decide to build her own nuclear shield? For the moment no clear consensus has emerged, although the second alternative would appear to be ruled out for the time being in Japan, and the third to be completely unacceptable.

Not a few people have argued that Japan should continue to avoid joining the arms race, seeking instead to make her contribution in other fields, for example, overseas aid and technical assistance. Even here, however, many of the other advanced industrial democracies have tended to be more generous, despite the fact that their economies have not been as successful as Japan's. Between fiscal 1978 and 1980, under very considerable external pressure, Japan doubled her Overseas Development Assistance (ODA) to reach 0.33% of GNP (compared with 0.47% average in the European Community). Most recently a new five-year programme to double Japan's ODA and also to increase the grant element of the aid has been adopted. Even so, by 1985, Japan's ODA will be average, it will not be outstandingly generous.

If Japan, therefore, seeks to make her contribution not in terms of military defence payments, but rather in terms of assisting the developing world and improving North-South relations she still has a long way to go – not only in increasing her aid contribution, but in explaining to the rest of the world what course she has adopted, and in persuading the United States and the European countries that this is a valid substitute.

3. TOWARDS BETTER COMMUNICATIONS BETWEEN EUROPE AND JAPAN

Misunderstandings, communication gaps and inaccurate national stereotypes are no doubt the norm in international relations. In the case of Europe and Japan, and to a lesser extent, the United States and Japan, these factors have played a particularly important role. The reasons why this was so in the past are not hard to find; when there is no necessity felt to learn about another country, then knowledge of it will be slight, and the images which are held of it will be subjective, emotional and extreme. Until very recently, this has been true of European images of Japan. Conversely, in Japan, where there was once a strongly felt need to learn about Europe, images were formed which were less emotive and closer to reality. Today, the situation has changed. Now that elements of the Japanese economy have begun to impinge upon the European and American economies, and now that Japan commands a sizable and growing portion of the world's wealth and trade, there are compellng reasons for Europeans and Americans to avoid letting past stereotypes guide their reactions to Japan, and instead, to find out just how the Japanese manage it. A communications gap is the result of either a signal not being sent clearly, or of it not being accurately received. In the case of Europe and Japan both factors are at work.

The zest for foreign knowledge and culture has been one of the strengths of Japan. But the time has now come to reassess this old priority and for the Japanese to ask themselves whether they have something more to contribute to the world than consumer durables. In the words of the business leader, Saji Keizō, introducing a symposium appropriately entitled *Japan Speaks:*

> Although Japan has become a major economic power in the world today, she has yet to express her unique cultural heritage in universal terms . . . If Japan is to find a viable role in the world community and contribute to the true progress of that community she must discover anew, from an international perspective, the essence of her own culture and national character. Japan must also develop the means and ability to express this essence'.[3]

At the very least, the costs of being misinterpreted or misunderstood by other countries have now become so high that a major effort to reach a consensus on Japan's world role and having done so, to transmit a clearer message, would appear to be only prudent.

It would be naive to assume that increased knowledge leads inevitably to increased understanding. Indeed misunderstanding and the consequent shocks which flow from it, may be the essential prerequisites for creating the willingness to learn. Nor do increased contacts necessarily lead to less friction or to better understanding – maybe even the reverse. Even so, it would be foolish not to attempt to strengthen and broaden our knowledge and contacts with Japan. Not only in the political and business world, but also amongst specialist cultural intermediaries in the universities or in the press upon whom we rely for accurate knowledge and information about Japan.

4. TOWARDS BETTER ECONOMIC AND TRADE RELATIONS
In the economic security sphere, it is vital for the Western European countries and Japan to ensure equitable relations with the developing countries, solutions to the oil problem and continued access to raw materials. None of these questions can be settled by Europe or by Japan alone, but they stand a far better chance of reaching a fair solution if Europe and Japan can act together. The same naturally applies to the maintenance of a free and open world trading system

and the necessary conditions for its continued functioning – a stable international monetary system and adequate safeguards, rules of conduct, and standards to guarantee fair play on all sides.

In bilateral trading relations both Europeans and Japanese (and the same applies to Americans and Japanese) could usefully take a number of joint actions which would contribute to lessening the heat and increasing the clarity surrounding their differences. These would include a dispassionate analysis of the trade frictions and their causes.

In the early days of the 1960s and 1970s, analysis of the trade frictions with Japan tended to be limited to the trade sphere itself. Mutual accusations were exchanged about tariff levels, trade practices or customs procedures. Next, when the improvement of such conditions failed to halt Japan's ever-greater export surpluses analysis turned to non-tariff barriers which supposedly kept foreign goods off the Japanese market. When this too failed to bring significant results the scope of the dispute was widened. Japan, it was felt, was enjoying a free-ride neither contributing enough to US military costs in the Pacific region nor to overseas development aid.

Various features of Japan's domestic economy were also held to explain why few if any of Japan's major trading partners could compete successfully with her in such key industries as steel, cars or electronics. These features included the distribution system, the more or less closed nature of the capital market, an under-valued yen, the Government-business relationship, and the supposedly closed nature of the large banking and industrial groups in Japan (the *keiretsu kigyō*). Others even complained of what they called non-specific barriers such as the Japanese language or a supposed national preference for buying Japanese machinery, despite the well-known taste for luxury western consumer goods.

A more positive analysis stressed selected features of the Japanese economy or society as lying behind the effectiveness of her industries, and so more attention began to be paid for example to industrial planning or enterprise management. Indeed there was a boom in books about Japan including a rather enthusiastic vogue literature on Japanese management systems.

It is now widely recognised that solutions to the trade frictions must not only include various classical trade policy measures but also a more effective reaction to the Japanese industrial challenge in Europe and America. Moreover, whatever the merits of the various analyses of the trade frictions, no single solution is going to fit the various problems in the different sectors. For example, however tempting, it is pointless for Europeans and Americans to believe that the root cause of the problem is the lack of openness of the Japanese market, or the under-valuation of the yen or for Japanese to argue that it is lack of competitiveness in European and American industries, or lack of effort devoted to exporting to Japan.

Take the case of automobiles. The background to the EC-Japan car problem is similar to that in many other industries: overwhelming Japanese strength in her domestic market followed by a very rapid expansion in world markets, including the EC. This expansion coincided with and in part contributed to a decline of the European industry, which, with increasing success, called for protection against Japanese imports.

Twenty years ago, the Japanese automobile industry was nurtured on the domestic market and grew very rapidly from an output of 400,000 units in 1963 to 4.4 million units in 1973, to 7.0 million units in 1980. Imports in the early part of this period were blocked by high tariffs. In 1963 Japan imported only 9,000 foreign cars. In 1973 the figure had risen to a mere 37,000. Automobile imports were liberalised in the early 1970s, but by then the costs of entering the market were so high, and the domestic competition was so strong, that foreign manufacturers did not consider it worth making the effort. By 1980 imports of foreign cars into Japan were not much higher, at 46,000 units, than they had been in 1973.

By 1980, thanks to a timely adaptation of their industry to producing reliable energy-saving cars, the Japanese had become the world's number one manufacturer and exporter of cars. In that year another record was broken in that only one car was imported into Japan for every 85 cars exported (compared to the EC figures with 1.2 cars imported for every car exported and the USA with six cars imported for every car exported).

Japanese wages in the car industry were above the European average by 1980 but about 10% below those of German car workers. Japanese workers also worked longer hours, were less frequently absent and took fewer paid holidays. Most important of all, investment in advanced technology and huge production runs contributed to the much higher productivity of the Japanese car industry compared with that of Europe or America. As a result the ex-factory price of Japanese cars was not nearly as high as comparable European and American models.

While the Japanese industry was gaining its lead in the 1970s, the European industry was already in decline. European car exports to the world fell by 30% between 1970 and 1980, partly because they could not compete with Japanese exports. This trend was very striking in the North American market. In 1970, European makers had a 68% share of the foreign car market there while the Japanese had only 28%. By 1980 the tables were turned: the Japanese makers took a 76% share compared with a European share of 21%. The same was true of other markets around the globe including East Asia. There the European share fell from 34% in 1970 to 20% in 1980, while the Japanese share increased from 58% to 70% over the same period.

In the Japanese market itself, European makers were only able to increase their share from 0.7% to 1.1% between 1970 and 1980, while Japanese makers increased their share of the EC market from 0.6% to 11.1% over the same period. Today, exports of Japanese automobiles to the USA and to the EC are under one kind of limitation or another and the bilateral automobile trade declined in 1981 for the first time in ten years.

The automobile case illustrates a number of points: the Japanese authorities protected ('nurtured') the domestic industry in the early 1960s from European and American competition. But European industry and governments only began to take notice and to put pressure on Japan to liberalise the market both for imports and investments when it was too late. By the time the market was liberalised the domestic industry was too strong to be challenged on its home ground.

The automobile industries in Japan and Europe are now adjusting to the changes in their power relations – increasingly, for example, Japanese makers have been investing in manufacturing in Europe, or entering into various forms of multinational production or marketing agreements. In this way, the sting may gradually be taken out of the bilateral trade tensions. But by now every schoolboy knows that if European makers wish to compete successfully with Japanese makers they will have to improve their labour productivity and increase their investment in new technology.

Automobiles are the biggest single component in Japan's trade both with the EC and the US but even if solutions are found to remove frictions and restore free trade in automobiles, there are many other sectors and products which will continue to cause friction and alarm. No one solution will fit them all but there are a number of actions which could be taken jointly or unilaterally in the EC and Japan which could lead to a much more fruitful adjustment of the economic relations between the two.

(i) Joint Actions
There is much that Europeans could learn from the Japanese in industries such as cars and electronics. Conversely, the Japanese could probably gain through technological cooperation in industries such as aerospace and pharmaceuticals. Such cooperation not only leads to useful cross-fertilisation, but it also brings European and Japanese industrialists and executives into more meaningful contacts than as distant observers of their respective government authorities arguing about the biscuit tariff in Geneva.

Technological cooperation, including joint research and development projects, could also prove extermely useful to both sides in areas such as information technology, exploitation of marine resources, biotechnology and new forms of energy. The basis for such cooperation already exists in various bilateral treaties and agreements. It only needs to be extended. Joint ventures between Japanese and European companies in third countries are a form of cooperation which has not always been happy, so far, but given time and patience on both sides, it could bring obvious benefits, particularly in heavy and capital industries including oil and mineral exploration.

Finally, both sides should continue to bring industrial and safety standards, including testing and acceptance standards in Japan and Europe, into line with the best international practice. Such standards should be introduced with adequate prior notification and mutual consultation and with regard for possible effects on international trade, including imports. Tests already conducted according to international norms, and certified by officially accepted agencies, should be recognised without requiring that they be repeated in the importing country.

Joint actions between Europeans and Japanese, at the level of government, industry or trading firm, already exist in many spheres. They should however be intensified. Not only are such actions beneficial in themselves, but they also serve to broaden and diversify the dialogue between Europe and Japan.

Because of the high degree of interdependence between the economies of Europe, Japan and the US, it would make sense on all major issues, not only to hold prior consultations on a bilateral basis, but also to give advance warning to the third partner or to hold trilateral consultations.[4]

(ii) European Actions
To complain that the principal cause of the EC's deficits with Japan was that the Japanese market has been closed to European and other foreign exports by tariff or non-tariff barriers is to ignore common sense and everything we know about the changing patterns of European trade. In short, the EC's exports to Japan increased during the 1970s at about the same rate as its exports to the rest of the world. So did Japan's exports to Europe. The difference was that Japan's world exports were increasing at twice the speed of the EC's. During these years the EC was securing declining shares in most Asian markets including Japan. The same was also true of the EC's share in developed markets such as the United States. And the reasons were the same: increased competition from Japan and the newly industrialising countries on the one hand, and on the other, the declining competitiveness of European exports.

This decline was brought about by low productivity in many key export industries such as textiles, steel, ships, cars and electronics. This in turn was the result of relatively low levels of investment over the preceding decade in new technology and equipment, ever higher costs of labour, as well as labour unrest. In short, the results of a decade of stagflation and economic malfunctioning in many of the European economies, whose extreme form, the English disease, at times showed signs of infecting the whole continent.[5]

Europe's share of world exports has also declined because a larger percentage of its trade is now concentrated in markets closer to home, in particular as the result of European integration within the EC. Even here, many of its key industries have only been able to survive because they have been protected from outside competition by one means or another, whether overt or concealed, direct or indirect. No amount of blaming Japanese trade surpluses or of protecting Europe's ailing industries will cure the disease. Indeed to do so can only prolong it by directing attention away from its root causes.

In the nineteenth-century, Japan first reacted to the western industrial challenge by shutting her doors and hoping the westerners would go away. When it was only too clear that they would not, the Japanese embarked on an all-out and carefully planned programme to learn what it was that had made the West so powerful and successful. They recognised their weakness and decided to catch up.

Today the tables are turned and Europe is faced with an industrial challenge from Japan. When this finally became clear in the 1960s, the initial reaction was negative. Now there are signs of a more positive approach, but it still remains to be seen whether this will lead to a carefully planned and sustained effort to learn what has given key Japanese industries such a competitive edge over Europe. And having learned the lesson, whether this in turn will stimulate changes leading to greater competitiveness in European industry.

Competitiveness in a given market today is the result of investment decisions and marketing strategies taken yesterday. The relatively poor performance of European exports to Japan, compared with Japan's exports to Europe in the 1970s and early 80s, was the result of decisions taken or not taken in the 1950s and 60s. But the same pattern need not be repeated in the 1980s and 1990s if the right decisions are taken now.

The Japanese have made perfectly clear what kinds of exports their industrial restructuring programme can lead us to expect. They intend to continue to move out of energy and labour-intensive industries into technology and knowledge-intensive industries – biotechnology, communications, micro-chip electronics, optics, computers, both hardware and software, numerically controlled machine tools, aircraft, satellites, medical equipment, pharmaceuticals and consumer durables such as video tape recorders.

Unless the Europeans can begin to meet this challenge by (i) restructuring their own industries in growth sectors of tomorrow and (ii) getting into the Japanese market now, they will find that the Japanese will take the lead in a select handful of the new industries in their own market, and then in the world market, just as they did in steel, ships, cars, bearings and home electronics in the 1970s.

A number of steps could be taken to prevent a repetition of the failures of the 1970s:

- Encouragement of much greater practical knowledge of Japan in Europe, including Japanese industrial and investment plans for the 1980s and 1990s;
- Encouragement of European investment in Japan including joint ventures and company takeovers, particularly for distribution, after-sales service and other infrastructures for the sale of European goods; and where volume is sufficiently high to justify it, encouragement of investment in manufacturing industries in Japan.
- Consideration should be given to manufacturing investment in relatively low labour cost countries (South Korea, Malaysia, Singapore) in order to export to the Japanese market;
- Much greater export promotion activities, especially of high

volume sales items to the Japanese market (it is after all not an isolated market in Asia but one of the world's largest markets);
• In a number of EC countries, chiefly Italy and France, there are about 50 quantitative restrictions against Japanese imports. In most cases these are relics of the 1950s and 1960s. Although discriminatory they are neither exclusively against Japanese imports nor do they cover items of any especial importance today. But in less than a dozen cases there are quantitative restrictions which are exclusively directed against Japanese imports and some of these actually cover major items (such as imports of Japanese cars into Italy which are limited to 2,200 per year).

To the extent that these restrictions have often been cited by Japanese negotiators as a major impediment to improving relations with the EC, and especially where they represent nothing more than a relic of the past, they should be removed as quickly as possible.

(iii) Japanese Actions
The majority of Japan's trading partners, including the EC, have a deficit in their manufactured goods trade with her. Most countries have no more than a one or two per cent share of the Japanese market in such huge sectors as cars, steel, ships, home electronics or tobacco.

Is everybody else out of step, or is it just possible that there is something on the Japanese side which has prevented greater foreign penetration of her markets? If the EC was the only foreign trading partner of Japan having a deficit with her, I would have long since concluded that this was solely the result of the EC's lack of competitiveness and general decline of interest in distant and difficult markets. Indeed this is precisely what Japanese spokesmen have often argued.

The argument would be far more convincing, however, if it were not for the fact that nearly all other countries appear to experience similar problems in the Japanese market, and not only in the industries in which Japan proved herself so competitive in the 1970s.

The heart of the problem lies in the Japanese import structure as it has developed during the post-war years. By the 1970s, alone of the advanced industrial countries, Japan was importing a relatively small share of industrial or manufactured goods, never more than 30% of total imports, and falling as low as 20% in 1975 and 22% in 1980 because of the higher bill for oil imports in those years. Most European countries and the United States on the other hand imported both absolutely and relatively a far greater amount of manufactured goods.

Since the EC primarily exports manufactured goods, and since 85% of its exports to Japan are of such goods, and since the Japanese market is protected against imports of agricultural goods, European export opportunities in the Japanese market are much fewer than in its own markets or the US.

There is of course, nothing immutable about an import structure. It results from a number of factor's chief amongst which are a country's endowment of energy and raw materials; its geographical setting and historical pattern of external trade and, finally, the industrial and economic policies followed by its government. Japan, like the EC, has very few raw materials of its own, so it has to import large amounts from abroad to keep its industries supplied.

Unlike most European countries, Japan has not been surrounded by equally advanced neighbours allowing the development of intra-industry trade with them such as is found, for example, amongst European countries.

All these factors encouraged a more autarkic development of Japan's economy than of most European countries or the United States. In addition, one of the aims of government economic planners in Japan in the post-war period was to reduce imports of manufactured goods and to build up a competitive manufacturing industry in Japan. Another aim was to maintain rapid economic growth. Both policies were enormously successful; amongst their results was an industrial structure heavily weighted towards manufacturing industries, including a number of world export leaders, and an ever increasing demand for raw material imports.

The other side of the coin was a level of manufactured imports far below that of her main competitors. Opportunities in European and American markets were therefore much greater for Japanese exporters than for European and American exporters to the Japanese markets. The Japanese were not slow to make the most of the opportunities which were offered. The result has been huge surpluses in her manufactured goods trade with both the EC and the US and with most of her other trading partners. Another result has been the very small shares achieved in the Japanese market by foreign exporters – either the advanced industrial countries, or the newly industrialising countries.

Because of the relatively small amounts of manufactured goods imported by Japan, there is little or no chance that the EC or the US will be able to increase rapidly and substantially their exports to Japan – unless, the objective situation in which Japan finds herself changes, or there is a major shift in Japanese economic and industrial policies.

Already there is recognition inside Japan of the dangers of increasing exports without increasing imports. Not only because this leads to friction with her trading partners, but also because it distorts the use of resources within Japan. (Consider not only the international effects but also far more importantly, the domestic consequences of Japanese protection of agriculture and the medium and small business sectors. Consider also the domestic political effects of the removal of this protection.)

For these various reasons, there is now a felt need to adjust the industrial structure so as to integrate the external trade of the country more into the international division of labour, allowing a higher ratio of manufactured goods imports where comparative advantage lies outside Japan.

This adjustment will be encouraged by the shift of emphasis in the economy from concentration on manufacturing industry to long overdue efforts to improve the quality of life – housing, drainage, roads, hospitals, parks and similar amenities. The political support for this shift will no doubt come from postwar generations more inured to the comforts of life than their elders. There will also be added emphasis on social welfare as the structure of the population tilts further towards older age groups.

De-emphasis on heavy industry, especially energy-intensive industry, coupled with slower rates of growth, will lead to a falling share of raw material imports.

Externally, the emergence of newly industrialising countries (NICs) in Asia (such as South Korea, Taiwan, Singapore and Hong Kong) at a time when labour costs are high in Japan and there is a need to switch away from energy intensive, high pollution industries, means that for the first time Japan has acquired neighbours from whom it makes good sense to import goods rather than manufacture them domestically.

Because the NICs can score where Japan is weakest, they will score first. Indeed this is precisely what has been happening in recent years. In 1970, the Asian NICs had only about a 10% share of Japan's imports of manufactured goods. By 1980, this had risen to 25% (correspondingly the EC share over the same period fell from 25% to 20% and the US share fell from 40% to 30%).

Increased imports from the NICs would be a welcome contribution by Japan, which currently imports far less both relatively and absolutely from them than does the US or the EC, although 70% of developing country manufacturing industry is situated in East Asia – closer to Japan than to Europe or America.

Apart from these major changes in the Japanese economy and industrial structure – which have already begun but which will take years to complete – a number of practical steps which would greatly assist European and other foreign exporters to the Japanese market are now being reviewed with a new urgency.

These steps include:
- Examining the possibility of removing the twenty-seven residual import quotas on farm products, leather goods and coal, as well as lowering tariffs on a number of products including computers;
- According treatment to foreign tobacco manufacturers in the Japanese market equal to that enjoyed by the Japan Tobacco Monopoly:
- Purchasing decisions of public corporations to be made open to foreign bidders;
- Foreign companies to be allowed reciprocal opportunities for takeovers, as Japanese companies enjoy in Europe;
- Foreign banks to be allowed the same operating conditions as Japanese banks enjoy in Europe; greater liberalisation and internationalisation of capital markets; full liberalisation of the insurance sector;
- Continued efforts to bring testing and approval procedures in line

with the best international practice (already mentioned where it more properly belongs under 'Joint actions');
• Strict enforcement of regulations governing the prohibition of import cartels.

On the export side, Japanese companies should avoid 'torrential downpours' of exports in particular sectors or particular markets. Such 'downpours' are more likely to happen because at the moment the modern sector of Japanese industry concentrates its efforts on a mere handful of export items – cameras, cars, electronics, ships and steel. The government could try to encourage a greater diversification of exports in order to spread their impact. It should also keep a sharp eye open and, if necessary, be prepared to encourage the continuation of the various kinds of export restraint which have been practised until now in potentially dangerous situations.

Pricing policies of exporting companies can also do much to reduce trade frictions. Prices should be adjusted, taking into account price levels in export markets and not, for example, adjusted as an immediate reflex to foreign exchange fluctuations.

In the 1960s, the Americans jumped the hurdle of nascent European protectionism by switching from exports to direct investment in manufacturing industry in Europe. By the end of the decade they were deriving far more revenue from their investments there than from their exports. These investments also provided a bridgehead for popularising American management methods and the American way of life in general.

More Japanese direct investment in manufacturing in Europe could possibly play the most important role in preventing trade frictions especially where such investment provides employment on a scale sufficient to take the sting out of the main accusation against Japanese exports, namely that they increase unemployment.

Those Japanese factories which have already been set up, for example, in Britain, which takes the lion's share of Japanese manufacturing investment in Europe, have created an excellent impression of Japanese management methods, and they have generally received a very positive press. The conditions for such investment usually include requirements to buy a certain percentage of local components, or to sell a minimum amount of the product on external markets. Such conditions may not be totally welcome, but the advantages in gaining local support may well prove to be the determining factor.

5. CONCLUSIONS

The joint actions to improve trade relations between the EC and Japan outlined above have no hope of succeeding, unless both sides are prepared to take the half dozen individual, but complementary, actions listed for each. Nothing can be achieved if both sides continue to put the onus to act on the other as they have done in the past. The Europeans, for example, blamed the Japanese for exporting with an unfair advantage, and for keeping their domestic markets closed.

Indeed so often was this latter reproach repeated that it is hard to escape the conclusion that in the minds of some, the old image of the Japanese as inscrutable had influenced the conclusion that their market was impenetrable. These critics, many of whom had never engaged in business in their lives, let alone in the Japanese market, rarely addressed themselves to the root cause of the problem in Europe, namely lack of competitiveness and failure to take the Japanese market seriously.

The Japanese, on the other hand, frequently blamed the Europeans for lacking the will to export to Japan and for protecting industries which were declining because of European laziness. They rarely acknowledged that the structure of the post-war Japanese economy was geared to a vertical division of labour (imports of raw materials/ exports of manufactures) rather than to horizontal division of labour with advanced industrial countries such as those in Europe. Nor did they recognise that Europe's greater integration into the horizontal division of labour with newly industrialising countries has meant that its labour-intensive industries have been placed under more severe strains than those faced by Japan, which until recently has been more isolated.

Both sides need to acknowledge their own responsibility for improving trade relations, and be able to take the necessary actions, confident that the other is doing the same. In doing so, full recognition should be given to the efforts of the other. To achieve these aims a broader political dialogue is required between Europe and Japan, and more efficient channels of communication than exist at present.

If we fail to take these actions, frictions between Europe, Japan and the United States will increase, thereby weakening our ability to cope with North-South or East-West problems. More and more trade will fall under one kind of protection or another and domestic and international political consequences will be disastrous for all three partners, particularly Japan and the EC, which in their different ways are heavily dependent for their prosperity on international trade. Above all, in Europe the will to respond positively to the great shift in the world balance of power, which the rise of Japan signals, will be undermined.

NOTES
1. H.A. Johnson and G.R. Packard, *The Common Security Interests of Japan, the United States and Nato* Cambridge Mass. Ballinger 1981.
2. International Institute for Strategic Studies, *The Military Balance, 1983-1984*, London, 1984.
3. Introduction to the Internatinal Symposium, *Japan Speaks* by Saji Keizo, President of the Suntory Foundation, Osaka 1980 – reprinted in the brochure *Suntory Foundation* (Osaka, 1983) p.1.
4. Mushakoji Kinhide 'A Note on Trilateral Crisis Diplomacy' 1973, is still highly relevant.
5. See for example EC Commission, 'The Competitiveness of European Industry' Brussels, 1982.

4
Psychological Aspects of Euro-Japanese Trade Frictions: A Japanese Viewpoint

YOSHIMORI MASARU

HISTORICAL ANALOGY

In 1911 a German economist wrote:

'... There are certainly industries which have been affected (by Japanese competition), but one should always try to see how far this is due to competition from Japan or from other countries. Naturally one cannot say that the Japanese methods of competition have always been nice and praiseworthy, but here again many complaints are simply too exaggerated and one-sided. Most of these accusations show a striking resemblance to those by the British against Germany whose value we know too well ... When the new era came German businessmen adapted themselves more speedily to the changing environment. Then England's popular press started to turn out poisonous and sensational articles against German competition. It is regrettable that part of public opinion in Germany attacks the Japanese in utterly the same way, and senses the yellow peril in every Japanese product ... What must be emphasised in Germany is this: our future requires friendly cooperation and not hostile confrontation and arrogant spite. For this reason, all those comments on the yellow peril are lamentable ...'.[1]

Let us look at the Anglo-German trade rivalry mentioned in this quotation, a rivalry which may be considered the first serious trade conflict of modern history. The setting was the Great Depression which began in 1873 and lasted until 1896. This economic crisis touched off mercantilism among European powers including Great Britain.

Anglo-German economic friction was basically sparked off by an increasing penetration of British home and colonial markets by German products. After her unification in 1871, Germany rapidly made inroads into Britain's industrial dominance. Between 1880 and 1913 British exports increased by 24% but Germany's nearly doubled. Britain's share of world trade declined from 38.2% to 27.2%, whereas Germany's grew from 17.2% to 21.7%.[2] Indeed, the rapid industrial expansion and overseas market penetration of a united Germany was the most important development of the half-century that preceeded the First World War.³

While Britain's hegemony as the world's largest exporter remained intact, one by one her traditional foreign markets were lost to Germany. In 1885 Germany replaced Britain as the largest exporter to Holland.

It was at this time that British manufacturers began to accuse their German competitors of 'unfair' methods which they allegedly employed: the German sold shoddy merchandise, often under the guise of British articles; accepted training engagements with British trading houses in order to spy out a particular trade; pandered to the tastes of the natives and seduced them by concessions to their ignorance – even to the point of translating sales catalogues into their language.⁴ In fact, British industry itself was to blame for its declining competitive edge against Germany. From the German viewpoint, Werner Sombart wrote in 1915:

> 'All reliable and authoritative observers appear to agree that today a condition of 'capitalist decline' has made its appearance in England. You may observe it in several ways. 1. The English businessman, unlike the German, has not kept pace with progress; he has not taken technical science into his service. Indeed, in the field of technology he is miles behind. The Englishman declares the adoption of the newest methods to be impossible. . . . As for his machines, they are ancient models of which he is proud; whereas in reality they are only fit to be thrown on the scrap-heap. . . . Then English packing cases are too heavy; the foreigner packs his wares lightly and according to requirement. The Englishman neglects the finish of his commodities, which is quite independent of the quality. He does not cultivate his advertisement. English goods are frequently of too high a quality and therefore too expensive. The Englishman forces his tastes upon the market; he will deliver goods in the way he thinks best, or not at all. 2. The spirit of enterprise, interest in business, and love of industry are all declining. The old business ideal is disappearing and a new outlook on life is taking its place.⁵

This Anglo-German emnity came to a temporary halt in the 1890's when British trade began to recover. Trade friction, however, cast a dark shadow over overall relations between the two nations, as a feeling of suspicion and misunderstanding remained between them. The Germans were annoyed that they were unjustly accused and took pride in the fact that the compulsory label 'Made in Germany' turned out to be a recommendation rather than a stigma.

JAPANESE-EUROPEAN TRADE CONFLICT

The preceding historical outline reveals remarkable similarities between the background, causes and development of trade conflict today and a century ago. After two world wars, industrialised nations seem to have learnt little about preventing, much less finding a mutually satisfactory solution to the problem. What follows is an overview of major factors responsible for the current trade dispute between Europe and Japan analysed from a Japanese point of view.

PROLONGED ECONOMIC CRISES

It is hardly necessary to say that today's economic friction is in general an important consequence of the global economic crisis triggered by the first oil shock of 1973 and aggravated by the second of 1979. Trade problems between Japan and Europe certainly existed before 1973, but it was in 1976 when a Japanese economic mission, headed by Doko Toshio, the then president of Keidanren, came to Europe that Japan began to be blamed much more loudly for the trade imbalances, particularly by Britain and France.

Today, all EC member countries are plagued by a worsening economic situation which in turn provokes social and political destabilisation. On the other hand, Japan's economic performance has been relatively sound, particularly in terms of her balance of visible trade. The Japanese situation is interpreted by her western trade partners not only as the result of successful adaptation to a radically changed economic environment, but also and particularly as a testimony to Japan's protectionist trade policies and practices, whether at governmental, industrial or socio-cultural levels.

DECLINE OF CAPITALISTIC SPIRIT IN EUROPE

'Capitalist decline', which Sombart diagnosed in British industry at the beginning of this century is now widespread in Western Europe, including West Germany. A similar symptom is also seen in the United States. Capitalistic spirit is defined as a set of businessmen's attitudes characterised by their drive and hard work for material and non-material rewards through innovation and expansion of their business activities, and by their willingness to accept accompanying risks and responsibilities.

The historical development of Western Europe demonstrates that rising welfare and affluence is at the same time a process of diminishing capitalistic spirit. As the first industrial nation, Britain was also the first to experience an industrial decline which according to André Siegfried started around 1880-85. The British historian Correlli Barnett also suggests that the current 'British Disease' dates back to about the same period and hence refers to it as a 'Hundred-Year Sickness'.[7] More recently, West Germany seems to have been caught in a similar phase. As a German sociologist says, 'the protestant-capitalistic-individualistic work ethic of the last two hundred years has come to a crisis . . . and it is probably not an exaggeration to say that this changing value system is comparable to the revolutionary shift from an agricultural outlook to a capitalistic-individualistic orientation.[8]

NATIONALISTIC REACTION

A trade conflict resembles a military conflict in the sense that both arouse strongly nationalistic sentiments in the countries concerned, but particularly in the one whose competitive position is threatened. Economic nationalism finds its expression in emotional accusations, unilateral and exaggerated statements and even insults voiced by journalists, businessmen and politicians against the foreign competitor.

In the way Europeans react to a trade problem, there appears to have been no substantial change over the last century since the time of the Anglo-German trade dispute. This is one of the crucial differences between Japanese and Europeans. While the post-war Japanese have lost virtually all nationalistic sentiments because of their pre-war and war-time associations, nationalism is still vigorous in Europe, at least in comparison with Japan. This is why Japanese have been unable to understand the emotional overtones of European arguments against Japan.

In 1978 former US special trade representative Strauss remarked that 'pressures' were necessary in negotiating with Japan. A recent publication by the French Government stresses that it has to negotiate with Japan 'in a spirit of great firmness – the only efficient approach to commercial strategy with Japan'.[9] This approach is shared at least by some European businessmen in negotiating with their Japanese counterparts. Some French business executives in Japan, for example, are supporters of this 'strong method' according to which the Japanese are 'Asians who respect force and to whom it must be shown at all cost, in order not to be eaten by them'.[10]

This tough attitude often takes the form of derogatory and emotional statements against the Japanese, apparently to inflict a sort of psychological shock. A case in point is the widely reported 'secret' document by Sir Roy Denman, Director of External Relations of the European Commission. The rudeness with which he described Japanese housing conditions and devotion to work provoked a wave of indignation[11] and protest not only among the Japanese but also among the Europeans themselves. Already in 1977 Takeyama Yasuo, Chief Editor of the *Nihon Keizai Shimbun*, described this kind of European attitude as 'dogmatic cynicism' in a series of articles entitled 'Arrogant Europe'.[12]

JAPAN AS 'SCAPEGOAT'

Today, most Japanese are convinced, rightly ot wrongly, that they are made scapegoats for Europe's own internal economic problems. Already in 1977 a high-ranking Japanese Government official, Masuda Minoru, then Vice Minister in MITI (Ministry of International Trade and Industry), said: 'Europeans find it politically convenient to blame Japan for their recession and unemployment problems . . .'.[13] Recently, Amaya Naohiro, former advisor to MITI, was writing about 'a hundred per cent "goatability"' of the Japanese, though he was referring to the US attitude. 'Goatability' is a word coined by the Japanese which is becoming increasingly popular. It denotes the easiness with which Japan is held responsible for economic problems in other countries.

Why do they hold such a view? Firstly, the Japanese often have the feeling that Japanese 'responsibility' for trade deficits, unemployment and other economic problems in Europe is deliberately exaggerated and that it does not correspond to reality. One such case is the accusation by the French Government in early 1981 that each Japanesee car imported created five unemployed. This was followed by a blocking of Japanese cars landed at Le Havre. The Japanese automobile industry felt that it was picked out as a scapegoat to serve the approaching presidential campaign. From the Japanese viewpoint, it was difficult to accept the blame, as Japanese cars represented hardly 3% of the total French market, whereas other imported cars secured over 25% of the market.

A more recent example is the decision by the French Government in March 1983 to concentrate all import and customs clearance procedures of VTR's in the small provincial town of Poitiers. Thanks to this incident, in Japan, Poitiers has suddenly become the second best-known French city after Paris. The French measure was understandably received with astonishment by the Japanese because of its spectacular, unilateral and abrupt nature. The French move was probably a definite confirmation of the already prevailing sentiment in Japanese business circles regarding French protectionism. It was an unfortunate decision, as the author's conversations with a number of Japanese businessmen revealed that France's image as a 'high-risk' country for direct investment was further reinforced by this measure.

During the EEC-Japan Trade Symposium held in London on 17 February 1977 a Japanese participant asked if the British reaction to her trade deficits with Japan was not exaggerated, given the fact that Japan only occupied ninth place in terms of its share of the UK's total trade deficit – after the Netherlands, the Scandinavian countries, the USA, Canada, Iran, West Germany, the USSR, and France. In replying, one British speaker, Roderick MacFarquar, replied that it was easier to raise issues with Japan than with the Common Market nations. As a second reason he stated that Japan, being a newcomer in the European market, was much less known and understood by Europeans. This kind of argument is hardly convincing to the Japanese and reinforces their feeling of being discriminated against.

Particularly caustic criticisms are voiced by European firms faced with internal managerial problems. Hans Thomé, a member of the Executive Board of Volkswagen, who was acting on behalf of sick president Toni Schmücker, devoted approximately 50% of his speech at the 1981 annual stockholders' general meeting to denouncing 'aggressive' Japanese competition. This attitude was widely interpreted by the Japanese automobile industry as an attempt to camouflage Volkswagen's substantially reduced earnings due to big losses in its Brazilian operations and, above all, of its Triumph-Adler subsidiary whose take-over had been initiated and carried through by Thomé himself. In October 1981 he abruptly resigned assuming responsibility for the failure of this acquisition.

Probably one of the most significant cultural differences between the Japanese and the Europeans lies in the attitude taken when faced with an error or failure for which one is responsible. The Europeans seem to protect themselves against possible criticisms or sanctions by denying their responsibility or even by trying to shift it to other persons or circumstances. In Japan, on the other hand, a fault in itself is not generally considered to damage one's credibility nor to necessitate any sanction, as long as one admits it and strives to make up for it. Japanese firms which are hard pressed by a foreign competitor find it more productive to take it as a challenge to be met, rather than to find fault with the competitor.

For the Japanese, it is unfair, degrading and even morally offensive not to honestly recognise one's weakness or shortcomings and to try to divert responsibility to others. The usual Japanese reaction to such behaviour is contemptuous neglect and silence.

Besides, the Japanese detest open and direct verbal confrontations, considering this as vulgar 'mud slinging' unworthy of a mature personality. They prefer silence to an exchange of harsh words. Seeking a scapegoat is thus a rare phenomenon in Japan. This point may be illustrated by the fact that the Japanese language does not have a word exactly corresponding to 'scapegoat', and that the English word is used particularly in the context of Japan's trade problems with Europe and the United States.

For these reasons, the Japanese have not taken European complaints too seriously and have contented themselves with taking measures grudgingly, convinced that these will never provide a final solution to the problem, but that the gesture would temporarily damp down 'noisy' European demands. According to Dominique Olivier, Director of the office Franco-Japonais d'Études Économiques, this passivity coupled with the neglect and silence with which the Japanese countered European accusations – which were hardly convincing from a Japanese viewpoint – has led to a European interpretation that Japan had in fact recognised its responsibility for the trade problems with Europe. This, in turn, contributed to a reinforcement of the European image of Japan 'as an ideal nation for a scapegoat'.

ANTI-JAPANESE FEELINGS

The ultimate expression of Japansese-European friction is anti-Japanese feeling among European trading countries. This antagonism is another expression of a mounting xenophobic tendency in Europe where the presence of foreign workers is large. Underlying this psychological climate is a worsening economic situation, particularly rising unemployment. Japan is more vulnerable to such hostile feelings because of memories of the last war, which are still vivid among many Europeans who are influential political and business leaders. While the Japanese consider it a virtue to 'wash away' the past and let bygones be bygones, wartime images and attitudes against Japan are perpetuated in Europe.

Some European journalists go as far as to use strongly racial expressions such as 'yellow peril'. Esteemed business executives refer to the Japanese as 'the Japs' even in public speeches. Gyllenhammer, the President of Volvo, reportedly used this word during a press conference regarding its Kalmar plant. Reminded by a Japanese reporter who was present, he switched to 'the Japanese' for about 30 minutes only to begin using 'Japs' again.[14] Arnold Weinstock, President of the British General Electric Company also called the Japanese 'the Japs' during his talk at a French business school in 1978. In the United States Congressman John D. Dingell was quoted as having referred to the Japanese as 'little yellow people' in a closed meeting on 26 February 1982.[15]

The Japanese of course, cannot be indifferent to this attitude on the part of a few but highly responsible European businessmen. Already in 1977 one of the best-known Japanese journalists, Takeyama Yasuo was criticising 'European cynicism towards Asia, prejudices and arrogance' and joined Ronald Dore, then Professor of Sussex University, who maintained that there was an element of 'yellow peril' feeling in the European reaction against Japan.[16] He was referring to a full-page article entitled 'Tora! Tora! Tora! Japan's Exporters Launch Total War' in the *Sunday Times*, 13 February 1977.

Indications are that the Japanese are becoming increasingly sensitive to the emotional tone of western, particularly US reproaches. Recently, for instance, two well-known Japanese specialists on American-English literature drew a parallel between increasing anti-Japanese sentiments in the US and the pre-war US attitude towards Japan, and argued that this played a major role in the enactment of the anti-Japanese Immigration Act leading to aggravation of Japan-US relations.[17]

Similar worries are expressed by Nikaidō Susumu, Secretary General of the Liberal Democratic Party: 'Opinions expressed about Japan in the United States are anti-Japanese. They give us the impression of the pre-war days'. Sony's Chairman, Morita Akio says 'Americans are trying to impose their own laws and their own ways of life on the rest of the world. . . . Things appear to have gotten as bad as they were on the eve of World War II. I myself am repulsed by it'.[18]

SOME SUGGESTED COURSES OF ACTION

Endymion Wilkinson, an EC-Commission official, has admitted with unusual frankness that 'there is absolutely no solution to the Japanese-European trade conflict as long as the Europeans do not recognise that Japan's trade surpluses with Europe are the result of the high quality and strong competitiveness of Japanese products. To hold the Japanese tariff and non-tariff barriers responsible for the European trade deficits is nonsense . . .'.[19] It is precisely for this reason that European businessmen are increasingly interested in Japanese management and that study-missions go one after another from Europe to Japan.

The Japanese-European trade friction, however, is not merely a confrontation of two sets of different business strategies, structures and environments, but more importantly it is a confrontation of two different civilisations with different mentalities, value orientations, work ethics, achievements and motivation. It is also an event of historical significance, as European civilisation is being challenged for the first time after the thousand years of global European hegemony which followed the repulse of the Arabs at Poitiers in AD732.[20] That challenge comes from Japan and it is an economic one. New European responses will take some time, while the trade problem urgently needs to be solved. Both Japan and Europe have to make an effort to overcome this problem.

For the Europeans:
(1) It is essential that the present trade friction should not be allowed to degenerate into an emotional and nationalistic confrontation. Should this happen and become a common practice, communication between Japanese and Europeans would become even more difficult. The likely consequences are clear from the history of international relations over the last century. As we move towards the end of this century, it is high time that economic problems were discussed and resolved with calmness and reason, and without verbal aggressiveness. One approach for the Europeans would be to set a time limit for the fulfilment of European demands by the Japanese. If they are not executed, the Europeans should simply take measures to solve the problem from their point of view. For instance, if a trade imbalance is not rectified within a certain period of time, Europe should limit Japanese imports. Though unilateral from the Japanese viewpoint, this mechanical and dispassionate method would be far better than prolonged negotiations which often escalate into an emotionally loaded exchange of accusations, as has at times been the case up to now.
(2) The Japanese are fully aware of the current economic plight of European countries. They also know that there is a limit, under such circumstances, to their exports to Europe. The European appeal to the Japanese should focus precisely on this point which is the most convincing and undisputed fact, rather than accusing the Japanese of 'protectionism'. As long as Europeans point out specific non-tariff barriers, the Japanese will work on them, but everybody knows that this will never be a final solution. The Japanese are much more strongly motivated to cooperate and help someone who straightforwardly admits his difficulty. A nation should no longer be inhibited about resorting to measures which are to safeguard its economy and its vulnerable sectors. When a nation is faced with a serious economic problem or too large a compettitive gap with foreign competitors, there is no other alternative but to close the door to foreign imports. This is after all what Japan practised until the early 1970s.
(3) There is a tendency in Europe and in the United States to link their trade deficits with Japan, with their demand that Japan should increase its expenditure on a military build-up. This argument, however, mixes an economic problem with a highly political issue. Revision of national defence policy is too serious a matter to be decided in a short period of time, as a national and probably an international

consensus would be required. In any case it will be some time before Japan can arrive at a clear position regarding its defence policy. Economic friction is an immediate problem and this is why Japan's security policy should be disengaged from the trade problem.
(4) Europeans view the Japanese basically as a menace, but it is an undeniable fact that a number of European products have successfully penetrated the Japanese market. Rather than being paralysed by a negative image, the Europeans would find it more rewarding and constructive to look at more positive aspects of Japan-Europe business relations. European firms which are successful in Japan should be asked to share their experience with others to stimulate their interest in the Japanese market.

For the Japanese:
(1) The Japanese seem to have overestimated the limit of tolerance of Europeans for Japanese products in Europe. That limit is being reached. They should realise that pure economic arguments, however valid, are not always practical in reality, particularly at a time of serious economic crisis. The Japanese should also realise that their overall image in Europe is still negative for the reasons which have already been mentioned. Self-restraint is an essential element in their further approach to the European market.
(2) The Japanese-European trade problem cannot be solved by a series of stop-gap measures to simplify or eliminate Japanese Goverhment procedures for imports. The importance of Japan's favourable trade balance with Europe as well as the serious economic situation in Europe oblige Japan to take radical measures. These should include, for instance, the fixing of Japanese currency parity with European and US currencies at a level which would give European and US products temporary price advantage over Japanese products. This currency manipulation should be ended when balanced trade with Japan is restored. Another policy would be for the Japanese Government to impose export surcharges on those products which are disturbing European markets.
(3) While Japan can be considered basically as an open market by European standards, it is true that there are still a large number of petty administrative procedures which hamper easy access of foreign products to the Japanese market. These bureaucratic obstacles help to create an image among Europeans that the Japanese market is not really open. Efforts in this direction must be expanded.
(4) Japanese Government and industry should substantially reinforce their efforts to inform Europeans regarding the real nature of Japanese-European trade friction and the various measures that they are taking to encourage European access to the Japanese market. It is important that such messages be addressed directly to the public at large through newspapers, magazines and other mass media. This is very important as it will counter European interpretation of this problem which is often incorrect and biased.

(5) From the business strategy standpoint, Japanese firms should now put more emphasis on the distribution of wealth among their employees, rather than the creation and retention of wealth inside the firm. More concretely, there should be more payment to employees and less accumulation of capital in the company. In any case, domestic and international markets are increasingly saturated. Japanese firms cannot continue to pursue their traditional strategy of unlimited increases of production volume at lower cost and greater market shares. Such a strategy is more and more dysfunctional in the depressed European market where there are very large numbers of unemployed. A rapid shift from capital-intensive to technology-intensive products is the most effective solution, not only to avoid further aggravation of Japanese-European trade friction, but also to spur chain-reactions of technological innovation, thus contributing to an economic revival on a global level.

CONCLUSIONS

International conflict is often the result of a change in the balance of military or economic power among nations. When this becomes prolonged and serious, frustration and anger tend to find their expression in emotional reactions, which are based on traditional stereotypes, regarding other hostile nations. In the case of the Japanese-European trade conflict, there is the underlying image of 'sneaky' Japanese who 'protect' their market by 'subtle' and 'unfair' administrative practices, or of 'egoistic' Japanese who accumulate wealth at the expense of the Europeans, and who are 'copying' European technologies, or of 'aggressive' Japanese whose ambition is to 'dominate' the world by their economic power. The economic threat from Japan overlaps the old European image of Japan, that of the 'yellow peril', a disconcerting term which is still used in Europe to the dismay of the Japanese. This old demon starts to appear every time economic relations between Japan and Europe become tense.

And yet the Japanese are a people just like any other. It is sad to see that some European and American politicians, businessmen, and journalists are exploiting the trade problem with Japan and are dramatising or distorting reality in order to advance their political or commercial interests. These persons are misleading and taking advantage of un-informed people. They are seriously hampering efforts for mutual understanding between Japanese and Europeans at the grass-roots level. They should be aware of the possible consequences of their actions in the light of what happened before the Second World War.

The mistake of the Japanese lies in their underestimation of the need to deploy vigorous but honest public relations activities to counteract such misinformation. The Japanese are already paying and will continue to pay dearly unless they do something very effective to remedy the situation.

Mutual understanding between peoples of different civilisations is a difficult task, particularly when they are burdened with a history of military confrontations. However, let this not paralyse the efforts of all those Europeans and Japanese who, despite their differences and trade problems, believe in their unity and their capacity for understanding.

NOTES

1. Karl Rathgen, *Die Japaner in der Weltwirtschaft*, Leipzig, 1911, quoted in *Frankfurter Allgemeine Zeitung*, 19 May 1981 (author's translation).
2. Michael Balfour, *The Kaiser and His Times*, London, Cresset Press, 1964, pp.48-49.
3. David S. Landes, *The Unbound Prometheus*, London, Cambridge University Press, 1969, p.326.
4. David S. Landes, *The Unbound Prometheus*, p.328 and Ross Hoffman, *Great Britain and German Trade Rivalry*, New York, Garland, 1982.
5. Werner Sombart, *The Quintessence of Capitalism*, London, T. Fisher Unwin, 1915. (English translation of *Der Bürger*) pp.150-151.
6. André Siegfried, *England's Crisis*, London, Jonathan Cape, 1931, p.22.
7. Correlli Barnett 'The Hundred Year Sickness' in *Industrial and Commercial Training*, October 1977. (London).
8. Martin and Sylvia Greiffenhagen, *Ein schwieriges Vaterland*, Munich, 1979; paperback, Frankfurt, Fischer, 1981.
9. 'Les relations économiques franco-japonaises' Conseil Economique et Social *Journal Officiel* 14 January 1982 (Paris).
10. Albane Callies 'Négotiations commerciales: les rencontres de deux modèles' *Revue française de gestion* September-October 1980 (Paris).
11. This EC document characterised the Japanese as 'workaholics' and described their houses as resembling 'rabbit hutches'.
12. *Nihon Keizai Shimbun* 25 February 1977.
13. *International Herald Tribune* 16 March 1977.
14. *Nikkei Business* 9 February 1981.
15. *International Herald Tribune* 25 March 1982.
16. *Nihon Keizai Shimbun* 25 February 1977.
17. Discussion between Saeki Shōichi and Watanabe Shōichi entitled 'Amerika wa "Hai-Nichi no Rekishi" ni Manabe' in *Shokun* (June 1982) pp.24-39.
18. *International Herald Tribune* 25 March 1982.
19. Endymion Wilkinson, *Gokai*, Tokyo, Chū Kōronsha, 1980, p.297.
20. Statement by Professor Robert Ballon at a Conference organised by Enterprise de Demain, at Brussels, 27 April 1982.

5
Japanese Security Policy and European Security

REINHARD DRIFTE

In the post-war years leaders in Tokyo have rarely perceived any link between Japan's security and that of Western Europe. Similarly, European security policies have generally been shaped with little reference to the Far East. Both these attitudes are particularly surprising as both Japan and Western Europe are geographically contiguous to the Soviet Union and both are linked to the United States by military alliances.

Several developments are slowly changing ideas in Western Europe and Japan concerning their mutual security interests. The relative decline of American power and leadership in Asia, against a background of increasing Soviet military strength and mobility, has prompted the United States to demand that Japan make increased efforts for its own and regional defence. A recent example is the idea of Japan defending its sea lane communications up to a distance of 1000 sea miles.

In addition, Japan has been asked to share some of the burden of worldwide western security. This proposal includes measures such as giving aid to 'strategically important countries' for example, Thailand, Turkey and Kenya. A further element is America's desire to make her numerous worldwide defence agreements more effective by creating various links between them. This policy has been assisted by the issue of the deployment of Soviet SS-20 missiles, and western economic sanctions against the USSR following Moscow's invasion of Afghanistan.

Below, I shall discuss the relationship between Japanese security policy and European security by outlining several issues of mutual concern. This will help to clarify the extent to which Japan shares Western perceptions of security, and how far domestic constraints allow her government to contribute to Western security.

THE EAST-WEST RELATIONSHIP

The most prominent issue affecting both Europe and Japan is the broad East-West relationship. However, as this is discussed in detail in Joachim Glaubitz's chapter I will limit my comments to three major points. First, there are common elements in Japanese-Soviet and West European-Soviet relations which may suggest the adoption of similar approaches. As has already been mentioned one common feature is territorial contiguity with the Soviet Union. However, whereas

Europe is contiguous with the USSR's most populous and important region, Japan borders on thinly populated islands and East Siberia which are little developed. This partially explains why Japan values China as a more important neighbour than the Soviet Union. Furthermore, Japan and China are linked by elements of cultural affinity.

Another common element is the Soviet occupation of European and Japanese territory. However, an important contrast between these cases is the fact that the Soviet-held islands north of Hokkaido no longer have any Japanese population. In Europe the Federal Republic of Germany has constantly to take into account possible Soviet retaliation against East Germans – in response to policies which might displease the Soviet Union.

A third point concerns the different importance which the Soviet Union attaches to Western Europe and Japan; with the former being taken far more seriously. Although this may hurt Japanese sensitivities and national pride it provides Tokyo with more leeway in its relationships with Moscow.

An issue which is closely related to the East-West relationship is that of arms control which first became an area of common interest, when the Nuclear Non-Proliferation Treaty (NPT) was tabled in the late 1960s. Despite elements of common interest it soon became obvious that cooperation in the field of arms control is inhibited by several – largely perception – related factors. One factor is that the United States is the only power which can deal with the Soviet Union on the same level, and arms control is basically a matter for the superpowers. Secondly, Europe and Japan both have regional outlooks whereas the United States has more of a global perspective on international security.

Other factors which inhibit a common approach to arms control by Japan and Western Europe are conflicting national interests on particular arms control issues. Finally, Japan has a relatively low interest in arms control when compared to Western Europe. The following cases are intended to illustrate these points.

When the NPT was submitted for signature and ratification both West Germany and Japan made similar criticisms of the inequality of its demands. The United States viewed, and still views, the non-proliferation issue from a global perspective. In contrast non-nuclear European states and Japan are concerned with their energy problems and wish to establish an independent nuclear fuel cycle. The United States is primarily concerned with the effect of advanced nuclear technology on the spread of nuclear weapons technology. Clearly, it is easy for the United States to adopt this view as it already possesses an independent nuclear fuel cycle. Nevertheless the NPT issue showed that despite common interests and concerns Japan and West Germany did not coordinate their policies since they had different views on how to use the issue as a bargaining counter with the United States.[1]

The most recent arms control issue is the modernisation of theatre nuclear weapons. Several years ago Japanese diplomats and politicians hesitated to engage in any meaningful dialogue on this subject when their West German counterparts first raised the issue with them.² Several factors explain this attitude. First, there is very great sensitivity in Japan towards any issue related to security or military matters. Ignoring such issues is considered to help in keeping aloof from external problems. Second, Japan tends to give exclusive conideration to the military equation between the United States and the Soviet Union – and has little interest in regional arms control. Finally, the constraining of Soviet power by mutually negotiated limitations and restrictions, as in the Helsinki process, remains an alien approach to most Japanese both inside and outside government.³

The possibility of the redeployment of Europe-based SS-20s to the Far East, as a result of Euro-American talks with the Soviet Union finally heightened Japanese interest in the modernisation of theatre nuclear forces. Until 1981 the Japanese Government had left any public protest against the installation of SS-20s in the Far East to its American ally. However, a more 'defence minded' public opinion in Japan, the presence of 144 SS-20s with 432 warheads in the Far East, the likelihood of the deployment of others to the Far East, and Euro-American pressure on Japan to support their position finally led to Japanese participation in the discussion of this issue.⁴

Until the breakdown of the Geneva INF negotiations in autumn 1983 the Japanese Government supported the so-called Zero-Option, since this was considered the safest way of preventing the redeployment of Europe-based SS-20s to the Far East. On his visit to Europe in January 1983 Foreign Minister Abe Shintarō stressed the importance of the global balance and expressed his support for the Zero-Option in Europe as well as in the Far East.⁵ During the Williamsburg Summit in June 1983, Prime Minister Nakasone, in an unprecedented step, backed the deployment of new Western missiles should the INF talks prove unsuccessful. Since the breakdown of INF negotiations both Japanese and West Europeans have urged the United States to find ways to reopen arms control talks with the Soviet Union.

Effective Euro-Japanese cooperation in this field is handicapped by several Japanese domestic constraints, which also affect other areas of common security interest. First, there are the three Non-Nuclear Principles which make it impossible for the Japanese Government to explain to the public that the danger of the SS-20s lies primarily in disconnecting Japan from the United States in a regional nuclear conflict. For the same reason the government is publicly opposed to the deployment of American nuclear weapons in Japan to counter the SS-20s, and to the presence of nuclear warheads on ships of the United States' Seventh Fleet. This is because the Non-Nuclear Principles do not permit the entrance of nuclear weapons on American ships into Japanese harbours where American naval units are stationed, or make regular port calls. However, since 1984 the US Seventh Fleet has begun to be equipped with Tomahawk Cruise Missiles which can be fitted with nuclear warheads.

A further complexity is that Soviet missiles in the Far East are not only directed against Japan and United States forces in the region. They are also aimed at China which does not wish to be a party to US-Soviet negotiations. Finally, at least until the autumn of 1983, there existed a temptation in Europe to reach an agreement with the Soviet Union – even if this meant the redeployment of Soviet SS-20s to the Far East.

THE MIDDLE EAST

The Persian Gulf is virtually the only region of the world where European, American and Japanese interests directly converge. Developments since 1973 have demonstrated that, in an emergency, Japan's pressing need for a stable supply of oil may prevail over domestic constraints in matters of security policy. This might well facilitate cooperation with other Western nations. However, there are even significant differences between the three as to how to maintain these common security interests.

Japan's general approach to diplomacy is primarily economic and this is also true of her attitude to the Middle East. In addition, this 'economic approach' also excludes the export of arms. Japan considers that direct Soviet intervention in the region is less likely than attempts to exploit political or economic instability. For this reason Japan is reluctant to support America's emphasis on a military approach – for example, her unsuccessful hostage rescue attempt in Iran, and the creation of the Rapid Deployment Force.

Japan considers that too much stress on military means may lessen the economic leverage which the industrialised democracies have on their adversaries, and could alienate friendly states in the Middle East. As a result, Japan has tried to associate herself with the West Europeans who have a more flexible approach to the region. This is also true regarding the Palestinian question on which Japan's position is closer to that of Europe than of the United States. On this issue Japan is even less inhibited than Europe since she feels no special obligation towards Israel.

Other significant differences concern ways and means of possible cooperation. Japan's constitution and public opinion do not permit collective defence or the dispatch of military personnel abroad, and it is debatable whether such action would be desirable. The Japanese therefore, have pointed out that some of the American forces based in Japan (which they support to the tune of $1 billion per year) are also deployed in the Indian Ocean for the security of the Gulf region. In addition, Japanese financial assistance to Egypt, to improve the Suez Canal has made it possible for large aircraft carriers belonging to the United States Sixth Fleet to pass through the canal.[6]

In 1980 the Japanese Government declared it constitutional to provide financial help for an international fleet which the United States proposed to create to deal with the Straits of Hormuz crisis.[7] At the beginning of 1983 the government indicated that it might make a financial contribution to the now defunct Western multinational peace-keeping force in Beirut.[8] This is certainly as far as Japan can go as regards military measures.

Another significant field of cooperation is increased Japanese aid to strengthen the political and economic foundations of Middle Eastern states. This approach is part of a new policy calling for aid to 'strategic countries' or 'countries bordering on areas of conflict'. This is part of the Comprehensive National Security concept which has developed since 1980.[9]

In the Middle East region, Turkey, Egypt and the Sudan belong to this category of privileged aid recipients. Unfortunately the international aid programme for Turkey provides a bad example of how cooperation with Japan should be organised. This aid programme was decided upon at the 1978 Guadeloupe summit meeting – from which Japan was excluded. Later, Japan was asked to participate in the scheme. Such incidents have left Japan with the impression that she is only consulted in times of need.

Other 'strategic countries' which have been aided by Japan include Thailand, Pakistan, Kenya and Jamaica. The latter two are particularly noteworthy as they were chosen by Tokyo to demonstrate its willingness to contribute – at least economically – to Western security, even in areas in which it has no direct political or economic interest. Japan has also given help to Zimbabwe to assist Britain's policy of establishing the country's independence. On the diplomatic front Foreign Minister Abe visited Turkey in 1983 to show Japan's recognition of that country's great strategic importance.

In recent years, Japan has repeatedly stated that she regards increased economic aid as an important element of burden sharing. So far her financial contribution to the Third World has been high in absolute terms, but very low as a ratio of GNP or in aid terms. Japan will attempt to double her Overseas Development Aid (ODA)-related budget in the 1981-85 period (as compared with 1976-80) from $1.7 billion to $2.14 billion – but will not achieve this goal, despite special consideration being given to increased aid.

The increase in Fiscal Year 1982 was 11.4 per cent, in 1983 24 per cent, and 10 per cent in 1985.[10] But Japan can at least claim that she has increased her aid at a time when most industrialised countries have been cutting theirs. This despite the fact that Japan has been affected by the recession, and her budget shows a record deficit. One might mention that West European countries could reciprocate Japan's help to countries like Turkey by making greater efforts in Asia – through such bodies as the Asian Development Bank.

THE IMPORTANCE OF TRILATERAL ACTIVITIES

While Western Europe is linked to the United States through NATO Japan is linked to the same superpower through the United States-Japan Security Treaty. However, no institutional framework exists for security cooperation between Europe and Japan. So far consultation and cooperation have been on an *ad hoc* basis or have taken place during the summit meetings of the major industrialised countries. The United States has been the most important promoter of trilateral consultation and cooperation in the security field, and thus has contributed significantly to bringing Europe and Japan closer together.

With its global outlook the United States considers that the linking of her major security alliances – in this case NATO and the US-Japan Security Treaty – is the best means of making these alliances more efficient at a time when American power is declining. In Europe, West Germany was the first country to begin a security dialogue with Japan, by signalling that the two nations had similar interests in the defence field. This idea was first voiced on the occasion of Helmut Schmidt's visit to Tokyo as Defence Minister in 1971. It was only in June 1978 that Kanemaru Shin, Director of the Japanese Defence Agency, returned this visit. Since then exchanges of high-ranking defence officials from Europe and Japan have taken place regularly.

The most important American private initiative has been the establishment, in 1973, of the Trilateral Commission; Japan has been a member since its creation and security issues are regularly discussed. Another private initiative has been a joint working group of the Atlantic Council of the United States and the Tokyo-based Research Institute for Peace and Security (RIPS) which published the results of joint discussions under the title *The Common Security Interests of Japan, the United States and NATO*.[11]

At the official level Japan has participated in the annual economic summits which have been held since 1975. Here, too, security issues are frequently discussed. The most remarkable such meeting was in 1983 when Prime Minister Nakasone supported the declaration which advocated the 'double track decision'.

Institutional links between Japan and NATO began in an indirect way with the visit of a North Atlantic Assembly delegation to Tokyo in May 1980. This was received by both Prime Minister Ohira and Foreign Minister Okita. Since 1980 Japanese parliamentarians have been invited as observers to the sessions of this NATO-linked institution. The Japanese Diet members who attend come from all parties except the Communists and Socialists. In May 1982 a Trilateral Security League of Diet members was established with nearly 200 members. In March 1983 it held its first meeting, in Tokyo, with 25 Ambassadors and Ministers drawn from 14 NATO countries.[12]

Direct contacts between the Self-Defence Agency and NATO headquarters in Brussels now take place regularly. The Japanese Government openly declares its appreciation of NATO, which would have been unthinkable some years ago. The Japanese appreciate the deterrent role of NATO and consider contacts with this alliance extremely valuable. As Tokyo has become more concerned with global security it sees NATO as an important source of information on security in Europe and its adjacent regions. Uniformed members of the Self-Defence forces also appreciate the increased status which stems from such contacts.

On their side Europeans seek Japanese evaluations of the situation in East and South-East Asia. When Canadian Prime Minister Trudeau visited Japan in January 1983 he even invited Japanese leaders to become more involved in the discussion of strategic affairs within NATO.[13] In the same year Japan's increasing contacts with NATO even led to erroneous newspaper reports that she had applied to join the alliance or become an associated member.[14] This was related to the question of sanctions against the USSR which followed the invasion of Afghanistan.

At a meeting held at Versailles it was decided to continue studies of these issues within the OECD, Cocom (Coordinating Committee on Export Control) and NATO. Since Japan is not a member of the North Atlantic alliance she insisted that she could not be bound by a decision taken in her absence. This clarification was particularly important for Japan as she opposed more drastic measures to curb the export of technology to the Soviet Union. Therefore Japan desired a more direct line of communication to the NATO Secretariat in Brussels.

At the same time, in April 1983, Japan began talks on security matters with Britain and France.[15] However, France remains strongly opposed to any direct Japanese link with NATO. In view of domestic opposition it is inconceivable that the Japanese Government will seek anything resembling an official association with the North Atlantic alliance.

Contacts have also been expanding in the military sphere. In September 1980 the Royal Navy conducted joint exercises with the Maritime Self-Defence Force for the first time. In February 1983 the first such exercises took place between Japan and France. When the British Minister of State for Defence, Peter Blaker, visited Japan in April 1983 he expressed interest in expanding the staff talks which have already been held between Japan and the United Kingdom.[16]

OBSTACLES TO A CLOSER EURO-JAPANESE SECURITY RELATIONSHIP

Recent developments should not mislead us regarding the problems which are involved in the Euro-Japanese dimension of Western security cooperation. Since Europe and Japan do not have a comprehensive relationship, like that uniting Japan and the United States, non-security issues will continue to dominate their relations.

The most important current issue is trade friction. This stems from the EC's balance of trade deficit with Japan of $11 billion. Although Japan's trade surplus with the United States is even higher Washington has a greater means of exerting pressure on Tokyo – or of securing trade-offs in the military or political spheres. One recent such example is the willingness of the Japanese Government to allow the transfer of military technology to the United States and the development of joint technologies between the two allies. However, Western Europe has been unable to sell weapons to Japan since American pressure has prevented this. France has been particularly outspoken in demanding that Japan buy European arms to offset Europe's trade deficit. As a result of a French initiative the

Commission of the European Communities has included this demand in its 'Revised List of Requests to the Japanese Authorities' of April 1984.

However, in the long run this demand seems likely to be counter-productive. Such sales would probably lead to the eventual abolition of Japanese restraints on arms exports, and thus provide Japan with another field in which to prove its competitiveness. That such a development is not desired in Europe has been made clear to Tokyo in a Franco-German joint note.[18]

Another fundamental obstacle hindering Euro-Japanese cooperation in the security field is the element of competition between Japanese-American and Euro-American ties. With the exception of the British and Germans most European members of NATO appear to have been rather hesitant regarding too close ties between NATO and Japan.[19] Each side is at times fearful that in a crisis the United States may be too busy elsewhere to answer its needs effectively.[20] Japan believes that the United States still leans more to her racial brethren, and regards American support for Britain in the 1982 Falklands/Malvinas War as an example. Europeans view the United States' increasing links with the Pacific with some concern, particularly as America now has more trade across the Pacific than the Atlantic.

Other obstacles to greater cooperation in the security field are simple differences of national interest. Apart from its different geographical interest Japan tends to be more accommodating to certain demands from the Third World. This is due to Japan's perception of her economic dependence and vulnerability. These differnt outlooks are readily understandable for in a crisis individual members of the EC can count upon some support from their partners, whereas Japan feels the danger of isolation. A recent example is Japan's signature of the new Treaty on the Law of the Sea (January 1983). Tokyo accepted this treaty so as to protect her good relations with raw material suppliers in the Third World. Different national interests also emerged in the Malvinas/Falklands War when Britain was supported by the other members of the EC but perceived Japan's response as slow and cautious. Japan supported the UN resolution which condemned the Argentinian use of force, but did not join the Europeans in their boycott of Argentinian exports. Japan merely took selected measures so as not to undermine the European boycott.

SOME CONCLUSIONS

Euro-Japanese security relations have developed considerably since the early 1980s. This has been due to Japan's changed attitudes concerning security issues, her better understanding of the global aspects of security, and the recent deterioration in East-West relations which has stimulated a joint Western response. Clearly, there are several limits to further Japanese contributions to Western security; these include the constitution, public opinion, differences of perception, different national interests and the lack of institutional frameworks for cooperation.

On the European side there is some hesitation concerning over-close security links with Japan. This has been particularly apparent regarding Japan's contacts with NATO. However, it is clear that no one would gain from any dramatic moves towards closer Euro-Japanese security links, since these would only stimulate counterproductive reactions.

NOTES

1. *Frankfurter Allgemeine Zeitung* 23 May 1969.
2. Department of State, Executive Seminar on National and International Affairs 22nd Session, April 1980. Robert Immermann, 'European Attitudes Towards Japan: Trilateralism's Weakest Link, A Case Study'.
3. For a detailed analysis of Japan's arms control policy see the author's contribution to J. Chapman, R. Drifte and I. Gow, *Japan's Quest for Comprehensive Security*, London, Frances Pinter, 1983.
4. *Frankfurter Allgemeine Zeitung* 14 January 1983.
5. *Neue Zürcher Zeitung* 6 January 1983.
6. Motoharu Arima, Draft of Speech to North Atlantic Assembly Session, 18 November 1982.
7. Interview with an official of the Japanese Ministry of Foreign Affairs, Tokyo 5 September 1981.
8. *International Herald Tribune* 31 January 1983.
9. For a critical evaluation of the Comprehensive National Security Concept see f.n.3.
10. *The Daily Yomiuri* 10 February 1984.
11. U. Alexis Johnson and George Packard, *The Common Security Interests of Japan, the United States and NATO* Cambridge, Mass. Ballinger 1981.
12. *Asahi Evening News* 11 March 1983
13. *Asahi Evening News* 18 January 1983.
14. *Le Monde* 11 March 1983 and *International Herald Tribune* 4 April 1983.
15. *Far Eastern Economic Review* 16 June 1983.
16. *Ibid.*
17. Commission of the European Communities, 'Revised List of Requests to the Japanese Authorities, Brussels', April 1984.
18. *Le Monde* 20 November 1981.
19. Immerman *op.cit.* see f.n.2.
20. Johnson and Packard, *The Common Security Interests* (see f.n.11).

PART III:

Japan, Europe and the Superpowers

6
Japanese-Soviet Relations in the Contemporary World

JOACHIM GLAUBITZ

At the beginning of the twentieth-century Russo-Japanese relations were already plagued by tension. As the two powers were unable to agree on spheres of influence in Korea and Manchuria, Japan broke off negotiations and in February 1904 her navy attacked Russian ships at Port Arthur. In the Russo-Japanese war which followed, Japan surprised the world with her remarkable victories. For the first time in modern history an Asian nation had defeated a European military power.

In September 1905 the Treaty of Portsmouth (New Hampshire) brought the Russo-Japanese war to an end. According to this agreement Russia ceded South Sakhalin, the Liaotung peninsula (in South Manchuria), and the South Manchurian Railway to Japan. Some years of improved relations followed but in 1918 Japan joined American, British and French forces in anti-Bolshevik intervention in Siberia. Seven years later Japanese forces finally withdrew from all Soviet territory, diplomatic relations were restored and Moscow recognised the treaty of Portsmouth.

By 1930 Japan's ambitions again seemed to threaten Soviet interests in the Far East and in 1931 her forces began the wholesale occupation of Manchuria. Within a year Japan had transformed these conquests into the puppet state of Manchukuo, and her armies sought further opportunities for expansion on the Asian mainland.

The Soviet Union reacted to this new situation with two policies. First, it proposed a non-aggression pact with Japan. Second, it strengthened its forces in East Siberia. In December 1932 Tokyo rejected the Soviet proposal for a non-aggression pact, and continued to strengthen its own forces in Manchuria. Tension on the Soviet-Manchukuo border intensified, and culminated in armed clashes at Changkufeng (1938) and Nomonhan (1939). Nevertheless, Japan's leaders sought to avoid an all-out war with the Soviet Union as their armies were already embroiled in a vast undeclared war in China.

News of the Nazi-Soviet pact in August 1939 came as an abrupt shock to Japan, for she feared that Moscow would use its new security in the West to exert greater pressure in the Far East. In fact Germany tried to convince Japan that she, too, should begin negotiations for a non-aggression pact with Moscow. This proposal received growing support among Japan's leaders for many believed that such an agreement would strengthen Japan's position *vis-à-vis* China and the United States. Consequently, in July 1940 Japan proposed a neutrality pact to the Soviet Government. This marked a major shift in Japanese policy and an agreement was signed in Moscow on 13 April 1941.

Two months later, in June 1941, the German invasion of Russia created a new dilemma for Japan's leaders. However, Japan did not enter the new conflict. Instead she decided to shelve plans for any attack on the Soviet Union until Moscow was compelled to transfer large forces to the European front. However, the outbreak of war between Japan and the United States made war with the Soviet Union unthinkable and Japan remained faithful to the neutrality pact.

In the end, it was the Soviet Union which terminated the neutrality pact on 8 August 1945 by entering the war with Japan, two days after the first atomic bomb had been dropped on Hiroshima.

Six months before, at Yalta, the USSR, Britain and the United States had agreed that Russia would enter the Pacific War 'two or three months after Germany . . . surrendered'. This agreement stipulated that South Sakhalin, and the Kuriles would be transferred to the Soviet Union.[1] However, the Kurile islands were never clearly defined in the agreement. In fact, throughout the post-war years Japan has claimed that four islands which are occupied by the Soviet Union are outside the historical limits of the Kurile chain.

In October 1956 when Japan and the Soviet Union agreed to resume diplomatic relations after the war, the territorial issue remained unsolved. However, at this time the USSR agreed that two of the islands (the Habomais and Shikotan) did not belong to the Kuriles and would be returned to Japan, as part of the negotiation of a future peace treaty.[2]

Within a few years the Soviet position hardened, this concession was withdrawn, and by the 1970s Moscow was insisting that no territorial dispute existed. The USSR now claims that her post-war borders are irreversible.

Against this unhappy background Soviet-Japanese relations have become increasingly tense in the past decade. The causes of this tension are many but to a large extent the Soviet Union is responsible for this trend. Since 1978 Tokyo has perceived the Soviet Union as a 'potential threat' to her security. But what Soviet action or inaction has brought about deteriorating relations with her East Asian neighbour? Three types of Soviet action have had a clear impact upon Japan:
(1) actions directly aimed at Japan;
(2) actions definitely concerning Japan's security;
(3) actions indirectly influencing Japanese policy.

Perhaps the most important action directly aimed at Japan concerns the territorial issue. Moscow continues to deny that any issue exists, and this denial remains the main obstacle to any improvement in Soviet-Japanese relations. Here, the USSR faces several problems. If she responds to Japanese demands she risks stimulating similar territorial claims in Eastern Europe. Furthermore, she would weaken her position in border disputes with China. In addition, loss of the disputed islands would deprive her of an important strategic position on the Okhotsk Sea, for she now controls its southern exit to the Pacific Ocean. Finally, given the bitter history of Russo-Japanese relations it is uncertain whether concessions on the northern islands would secure any significant degree of Japanese friendship.

The official Japanese position on the territorial issue remains uncompromising. In January 1981 the Japanese Government decided to declare 7 February 'Northern Territories Day'. This recalls the signing of the Treaty of Shimoda by Japan and Czarist Russia on 7 February 1855. In this treaty the two parties agreed that their frontier would run between the Russian island of Urup and the Japanese island of Iturup (Etorofu). In Tokyo this treaty is regarded as historic proof that the islands South of Urup, which the Soviet Union has occupied since 1945, have never legally belonged to Russia.

Behind Tokyo's decision to establish a 'Northern Territories Day' is the intention to transform the Japanese claim from a local demand to a nationwide movement. Inevitably the Soviet Union reacted strongly to 'Northern Territories Day', calling it a provocative decision and a return to Japan's militarist, expansionist past.[3]

Among Soviet activities directly aimed at Japan one must include military actions on the disputed northern islands. Since the summer of 1978 the USSR has deployed military forces on three of the four islands. According to Japanese sources the strength of these units is approximately one division.[4] This Soviet action can be interpreted as a reaction to the conclusion of the 1978 Sino-Japanese Peace and Friendship Treaty. On the other hand this treaty provided the Soviet Government with a welcome pretext to further strengthen its military presence in the North Asian-Pacific area, and to emphasise that the islands are now an inseparable part of Soviet territory.

According to the Japanese Defence Agency's annual *Defence of Japan* Soviet policy regarding the 'Northern Territories' is aimed at impressing upon Japan the inevitability of accepting the illegal occupation of the islands as a *fait accompli*.[5] The Japanese Government considers this development an 'increased potential threat' to Japan.[6] No relaxation of Soviet attitudes is apparent. Indeed, in the autumn of 1983 the Soviet Union further strengthened its air units on Etorofu by stationing over 20 Mig-23 fighters there.[7]

Besides deploying forces on Etorofu, Kunashiri and Shikotan the USSR engages in further military activities directly aimed at Japan. Soviet military aircraft directly approached Japanese airspace 285 times in 1983 and Japanese sources have reported a growing number of such incidents in recent years.[8] Among the developments which are of greatest concern to Japan's security is the increasing strength of the Soviet Pacific fleet stationed at Vladivostok, and its presence in the Pacific and Indian Oceans.

This fleet has been considerably reinforced since the early 1970s. In 1983 it consisted of 810 naval vessels of 1.6 million tons and 330 combat aircraft, including approximately 130 bombers. Since mid-1979 the 36,000 ton aircraft carrier *Minsk* has been deployed in the Far East; in 1983 about 60 *Backfire* medium range supersonic bombers (of the naval and airforce versions) based at two military airfields in the Far East, were assigned to the Soviet Pacific Fleet.

In recent years the Pacific Fleet's 24 SSBN submarines equipped with nuclear ballistic missiles have been replaced by a more modern version, the D-class SSBN.[9] The USSR keeps 20 to 30 surface ships from the Pacific fleet permanently stationed at Cam Ranh Bay in Vietnam.[10] This enables the Soviet Union to demonstrate its military strength in order to intimidate Japan. At the same time the USSR poses a potential threat to the important sea lanes of Japan and other Western powers which link them to South-East and East Asia.

The Japanese public seems well aware of the Soviet military threat. In 1983 when people holding the view that Japanese-Soviet relations were bad were asked why 25 per cent mentioned the military background of Soviet foreign policy; 54 per cent mentioned the Soviet position on the territorial problem.[11]

The USSR links its military activities around Japan with Tokyo's alliance with the United States. This tactic and the use of political and military pressure on Japan are Soviet methods of trying to instigate internal Japanese opposition to the US-Japan Security alliance. The Soviet Union has for years tried to drive a wedge between Japan and the United States – since its aim is to isolate Japan and – according to US Secretary of Defence, Caspar Weinberger – to 'prevent Japan from increasing its contribution to Western Security in peacetime', and in the event of war to 'preclude Japanese participation in a war in Asia'.[12]

So far the Soviet Union has not succeeded in this. In fact a large proportion of the Japanese public supports the Japanese Government in its policy of maintaining close relations with the United States. In an opinion poll conducted in June 1983 Japanese were asked with which countries Japan should maintain close and trusting relations. Of those polled, 39 per cent replied 'the United States' 17 per cent 'China' and only 3 per cent 'the USSR'. When asked the reasons for their views 38 per cent mentioned the security guaranteed by Japan's alliance with the United States.[13]

Nevertheless, there is latent uneasiness in Japan regarding too close a military alliance with the United States. This became apparent during Prime Minister Nakasone's visit to the United States in 1983 when he talked of Japan becoming 'an unsinkable aircraft carrier' and the United States and Japan 'sharing a common destiny'. These expressions were strongly criticised in the Japanese press.[14]

By and large Soviet policy towards Japan since the early 1970s has helped to intensify the military relationship between Washington and Tokyo. Despite many frictions this trend was accelerated by other Soviet activities, far from Japan, which were perceived in Tokyo as potential threats to Japanese interests. These include the Soviet invasion of Afghanistan, Soviet support for Vietnamese intervention in Cambodia and Moscow's interference in Poland's domestic politics.

Considering Japan's earlier policy of a 'low profile' she reacted to these events with greater decisiveness than might have been expected. In fact, her previous 'omnidirectional peace diplomacy' (*zenhōi heiwa gaikō*) has been replaced by a line which follows that of the Western industrial democracies increasingly closely. This change has found its expression in a foreign policy guideline which is said to have been formulated by Chief Cabinet Secretary Miyazawa Kiichi, 'Defending the Common Values of the Industrialised Democracies'.[15] This policy has been continued with even greater vigour under the premiership of Mr Nakasone.

This shift to a new principle in Japanese foreign policy must be seen against its historical background. For almost thirty years Japan was only marginally involved in the East-West confrontation. This confrontation has always had its main focus in Europe where two military alliances, and systems of social values confront each other, and American and Soviet ground forces are stationed in close proximity to each other.

This is not the case with Japan. Tokyo maintains a Security Treaty with the United States and it is this bilateral relationship which by guaranteeing Japan's security constitutes the basis of her foreign and security policy.

For decades the United States was the unchallenged power in the Asia-Pacific region, and no significant Soviet naval power existed there until very recently. America's deep involvement in Indo-China and the psychological impact of its failure marked a turning point in US power in the Asian-Pacific region. Meanwhile the USSR expanded its Pacific fleet impressively and deployed forces in various areas of the Soviet Far East. According to Japanese reports, since 1976 the Soviet Union has added 135 systems of SS-20 medium range nuclear missiles to its military build-up in Siberia.[16]

As a result of these developments the Asian-Pacific region is rapidly becoming a region of Soviet-American rivalry. Due to its geopolitical situation and its alliance with the United States Japan cannot avoid becoming involved in this rivalry.

Now Japan is already more deeply involved in the East-West confrontation than ever before. The time of trying to balance her relations with Peking and Moscow has passed and so has the era of avoiding clear political commitments to the United States and its allies. Japan's diplomacy has now developed a more distinct profile. As a Tokyo-based Research Institute put it 'Japan for the first time came out as a self-proclaimed 'member of the West'.[17]

The Soviet invasion of Afghanistan marked a turning point in Tokyo's attitude towards Moscow. The consequences of this drastic change are obvious. Against all expectations Japan vigorously and unrelentingly supported and imposed sanctions against the USSR after its intervention in Afghanistan. These sanctions included restrictions on exchanges of visitors and economic measures against the joint development of Siberia. Tokyo did not change its attitude until it realised that some industrialised countries in Western Europe were attempting to benefit from Japan's restrictions on her relations with the USSR.

In early September 1980 the Japanese Government decided to extend credits once more to the Soviet Union for two projects which had initially been blocked as a result of the Soviet invasion of Afghanistan. The Government also extended credits to the Export-Import Bank for additional financing of the coal extraction plant in South Yakutia, and for the third phase of the Siberian wood development scheme.

The Japanese Government justified its decision by stating that both projects were merely concerned with the extraction of raw materials and had no connection with military issues. Furthermore, these projects had been agreed upon prior to the invasion of Afghanistan. Japan is naturally interested in the development and extraction of raw materials in Siberia for its own benefit. In autumn 1980 Japan emphasised that its basic attitude on the issue of economic sanctions was unchanged. The question of whether credits for further economic cooperation projects with the USSR would be extended would be decided on a case by case basis.[18]

A Japanese Foreign Ministry official declared that the development of Siberia was not only in the interest of the USSR but also in that of Japan. He stated: 'We must do the minimum required to ensure our (economic) security by securing energy supplies.[19]

Japanese business circles opposed the economic measures against the Soviet Union and urged the government to mitigate its sanctions policy. Pressure on Tokyo was in fact increased by the attitudes of some Western countries which made it impossible for Japan to fully maintain its sanctions.

The French company Creuzot-Loire took over a contract worth $350 million for the construction of an electro-magnetic steel sheet plant which had originally been awarded to a Japanese-American group. The German company Hoechst AG, is said to have signed a contract for the construction of a polyester factory because the Japanese group of companies, which had already been awarded the contract was not prepared to grant financial aid of $200 million.[20]

After these negative experiences the Japanese Government's decision to extend credits to the USSR for the West Siberia-Europe natural gas project (worth $10 billion) was hardly surprising. The USSR intended to order $3 billion worth of equipment, steel pipes and other materials from Japan.[21]

Tokyo and Moscow also managed to agree on Japan being supplied with natural gas from Sakhalin. In early 1981 the Soviet Deputy Minister of Commerce visited Japan and negotiated an agreement for the Soviet Union to supply Japan with 3,000,000 tons of natural gas each year, beginning in 1985 or 1986.[22] According to Japanese estimates the demand for credits will reach approximately $3.5 billion. This will have to be raised by loans from the Export-Import Bank and other sources.[23]

During 1981 Japan handled her sanctions against the Soviet Union with increasing flexibility. In view of the relaxed attitude of West Europeans towards sanctions this was only to be expected. In the middle of 1981 the Japanese Government hinted that it was considering granting so-called flexible loans from the Exim-Bank to Japanese exporters. These loans had been terminated from the beginning of 1980. The Exim-Bank was permitted to begin negotiations with the USSR on financing the export of large steel pipes. The supply of these pipes for the natural gas pipeline is the largest pending project in which both West European and Japanese companies are participating.

The role of the Exim-Bank is to finance the delivery to the Soviet Union of 750,000 tons of large diameter steel pipes (56"/1.42 metres). In July 1981 Japanese private banks granted the USSR the first part of a loan of $400 million at an interest rate of 7.75 per cent over five years. In December 1981 another portion of Yen credits worth approximately $380 million was granted to the Soviet Union on the same conditions. According to a mutual agreement Japan had until the end of March 1982 to deliver 750,000 tons of steel pipes, and until the end of 1982 to deliver a further 700,000 tons.[24]

The proclamation of martial law in Poland on 13 December 1981 again strained Japanese-Soviet relations. Tokyo criticised Soviet interference in Poland's internal affairs. On the question of economic sanctions against the Soviet Union Japan did not immediately follow the United States, but carefully watched West European reactions. On 14 January 1982 one month after the proclamation of martial law in Poland the Japanese Government began to study a concrete six-point plan for economic sanctions against the USSR. According to this Japan was to step up the measures it had been taking against the Soviet Union since the invasion of Afghanistan, and take some new additional measures.[25] Finally, on 23 February 1982 the Japanese Government decided to take the following four comparatively mild steps:

(i) The indefinite postponement of annual official trade talks with the USSR
(ii) Postponement of the regularly held consultations on scientific and technical cooperation which would in practice lead to a reduction of the scientific exchange programme.
(iii) A refusal of the Soviet request to establish trade missions in cities other than Tokyo.
(iv) A warning to officials to stop issuing preferential visas for Soviet businessmen.

In comparison with the measures which the Japanese Government had discussed in January 1982 these measures were insignificant. Obviously, Japanese trading circles were concerned at the likely effects of possible sanctions such as the suspension of the extension of export credit loans. They feared that Japanese exports to the USSR might be affected on a large scale.

In 1982 the value of Japanese exports to the USSR was approximately $3.9 billion, that is a little over 2 per cent of Japan's total exports. Surprisingly, Japan's exports to the USSR in 1982 showed an increase of 19.7 per cent over the previous year. Japan's imports from the Soviet Union were a good deal lower. They reached only $1.6 billion, a fall of 16.5 per cent from 1981.[26]

Because of Tokyo's reluctance to implement sanctions against the USSR, Washington has asked her to join in restricting credits to Moscow. US Vice President Bush met Prime Minister Suzuki in late April 1982 and urged Japan to support the American proposal to tighten regulations on Western countries new credit offers to the Soviet Union. Vice President Bush proposed that the United States, Japan and Western Europe should discuss the issue at the Versailles economic summit in June of that year.

Prime Minister Suzuki supported concerted action against the USSR in principle. However, he asked Vice President Bush to exempt the Japan-USSR natural gas and oil exploration project off Sakhalin from sanctions. He contended that action against this project would do more damage to Japan than the Soviet Union.[27]

Despite Japan's severe condemnation of Soviet international behaviour its interest in continuing economic relations with the USSR remains strong. The same can be said of the Soviet Union. Both sides are also interested in improving their political relations. Japan wishes to establish a link between a significant improvement in economic cooperation and progress on the territorial dispute. However, Moscow wishes to separate economic and political problems.

The visit of a Japanese trade mission to the USSR in February 1983 led by Nagano Shigeo shows that Soviet-Japanese economic relations still have to overcome many obstacles. Japanese press reports generally denied that the visit had produced any concrete results – except the agreement to hold the next meeting in Tokyo in April 1984. On the other hand the official Soviet news agency, Tass, reported that the mission had signed contracts worth more than $500 million.[28]

Nevertheless Japan's reluctance, for political reasons, to extend economic cooperation with the USSR is obvious. Since 1978, the year of the Sino-Japanese Peace and Friendship Treaty, which was signed despite Soviet protests, Japan has rapidly extended cooperation with China. Until 1977 Japan's trade with China and the USSR were roughly equal – a value of $3.3 billion with each of the two communist states. However, Sino-Japanese trade reached $10 billion in 1983 whereas that with the Soviet Union was less than half this figure. Furthermore in March 1984 the Japanese Government extended another official loan of $2.09 billion to China. Together with the first loan to China of $1.3 billion which was agreed upon in 1979 this made the People's Republic the biggest single recipient of official Japanese credits. This Japanese shift towards Beijing had a political and strategic background. China supported Tokyo's foreign and security policy whereas these were attacked by the Soviet Union.

The discussion of defence in Japan which has become more open in recent years, is centred upon the issue of what additional efforts Japan should make within the framework of the US-Japan alliance. Such discussions have been approved by China but bitterly condemned by the USSR. Visits made by heads of the Defence Agency to NATO, Japanese participation in international military manoeuvres, official contacts between Japanese and South Korean defence officials and Sino-Japanese military contacts have all given Soviet commentators occasion to portray Japan as a power capable of creating instability in East Asia – primarily as an instrument of American strategy rather than as an independent actor.

China, however, with its basically positive attitude towards Japan, won the support of its highly industrialised neighbour – against Soviet competition – for its ambitious programme of modernisation. The problem of the deployment of Soviet SS-20 missiles in Siberia which only appeared in 1982 provided a further field of Sino-Japanese cooperation. On several occasions both Tokyo and Beijing agreed that the SS-20s deployed in Siberia are a threat to Asia.

The coincidence of strategic interests between Washington, Tokyo and Beijing, and their sharing of attitudes critical of the USSR with ASEAN, Australia, New Zealand and South Korea have forced Moscow to recognise that it has little leeway at present to extend its influence in the Asia-Pacific region. These conditions are also likely to continue into the foreseeable future. The causes of this situation lie primarily in Soviet policies towards Asia.

How the Soviet Union will respond in the long run to this Asia-Pacific grouping is uncertain. So far it appears that Moscow is reacting to this perceived threat by building up its forces in the Far East. If, in parallel with this, one observes America's determination to remain firmly committed to the Asia-Pacific region it appears that developments in East Asia show all the attributes of an accelerating arms race. This development will inevitably aggravate East-West tensions in Asia. In other words the Asia-Pacific region is developing into another focus of Soviet-American confrontation. For Japan – the closest ally of the United States – this change could create serious problems; for the United States will continue to ask Japan to shoulder a larger part of their joint defence burden.

However, the Kremlin has learned in Europe that industrialised democracies can encounter serious domestic difficulties if they are pressed to spend more on arms in order to maintain the so-called balance of power, and if they fear that their alliance with America will automatically involve them in a possible conflict between the United States and the Soviet Union. Soviet strategy aims at fostering similar fears in Japan so as to stimulate anti-American and neutralist tendencies and ultimately weaken the alliance between Tokyo and Washington. It remains to be seen how effective this strategy will be.

NOTES

1. The Yalta Agreement concerning the Kuriles and Soviet entry into the war against Japan is reprinted in J.A.S. Grenville, *The Major International Treaties, 1914-1973, A History and Guide with Texts*. London, Methuen, 1974. p.230.

2. *Pravda* 20 October 1956.
3. *Izvestia* 6 February 1981
4. Research Institute for Peace and Security, *Asian Security 1983* Tokyo, 1983, p.86.
5. Japanese Defence Agency, *Defence of Japan 1981*, Tokyo 1981, p.83.
6. *Ibid* p.85.
7. *The Japan Times* 11 March 1983, Kyōdo in English in *Summary of World Broadcasts;* FE 7452/A2/1 30 September 1983.
8. *Defence of Japan 1981 Defence of Japan 1983*, p.37.
9. *Asian Security 1982* p.57. *Asian Security 1983*, pp.86-88. *The Japan Times* 11 March 1983.
10. *Asian Security 1982* p.57
11. *Seron Chōsa* Shōwa 58/11 (November 1982) p.13.
12. *The Japan Times* 11 March 1983.
13. *Seron Chōsa* Shōwa 58/11 (November 1982) p.6.
14. *Asahi Evening News* 20 January 1983, *Far Eastern Economic Review*, 3 February 1983, pp.10-12.
15. *The Japan Times* 6 July 1981.
16. Dieter Heinzig, 'SS-20 in Asien (I)' *Daten, Aktuelle Analysen* Nr.6/1984, 5 February 1984, Federal Institute of International and East-European Studies, Cologne.
17. *Asian Security 1981* p.21.
18. *Japan Economic Journal* 9 September 1980
19. *The Japan Times* 9 September 1980.
20. *Neue Zürcher Zeitung* 25 November 1980.
21. *The Japan Times* 30 November 1980.
22. *The Japan Times* 28 January 1981.
23. *Asahi Evening News* 1 July 1981.
24. *Asahi Evening News* 11 July 1981, *Neue Zürcher Zeitung* 15 July 1981 and 2 December 1981.
25. *Nihon Keizai Shinbun* 15 January 1982 in United States Embassy, Tokyo: *Daily Summary of the Japanese Press* 22 January 1982, p.9.
26. *Sekai Shūhō*, Tokyo, 15 February 1983 p.31.
27. *The Japan Times* 25 March 1982.
28. *The Japan Times* 12 March 1983.

7
Regional policies in Europe and East Asia

WOLF MENDL

It is a paradox of our time that the real influence of the two giant states which have been at the centre of international politics since the end of the Second World War is declining. In fact, it can be argued that their ability to dominate events has always been exaggerated because their overwhelming military power has locked them into a mutually inhibiting confrontation. The catastrophic consequences of an open war between them has prevented each from making a bid for world domination, yet they are unable to overcome their deep-rooted antagonism so as to establish an effective condominium and impose a new international order on the world.

They cannot control the behaviour of their respective allies nor curb the revolutionary ferment of the Third World. In this situation of prolonged stalemate between the superpowers, reflected in a pattern of alternating periods of tension and *détente*, the major states at each end of the Soviet empire are endowed with a new significance which is driving them to re-examine their basic policies.

THE OPTIONS

For Japan and the nations of Western Europe the easy relationship with the United States has gone for good. Hitherto they have been able to count on a high degree of American tolerance and on the assurance that whatever they did would not undermine or destroy the protective cover of their alliance with the United States. Thus, they have pursued essentially nationalist policies under a barrage of protestations of loyalty to the 'alliance'.

France was at one end of the spectrum of 'independence', being most vocal and emphatic in distancing itself from the United States over specific issues. Japan has been at the other extreme being most closely identified with American policies, at least until the 1970s. West Germany and Britain were somewhere between; with the Germans nearer the French end – through their own 'special relationship' with France and their policies towards Eastern Europe, and the British nearer the Japanese position, placing great stress on their historic and 'special' relationship with the United States.

In the 1970s however, the environment in which the post-war alliances operated changed fundamentally. This was the result of the nuclear balance between the superpowers, Soviet ability to project military force far beyond the Eurasian landmass. America's humiliation in Vietnam coupled with a decisive shift away from the East Coast domination of American politics – and a growing preoccupation with the 'threat' on the southern flank. If Europeans and Japanese want to retain the system which has served their intersts so well in the past, the Americans will expect them to become more self-reliant within their own regions and more supportive of the United States in the rest of the world.

I have discussed elsewhere the options facing Japan and the major states of Western Europe under these circumstances.[1] They may choose to become gradually integrated into an American-led global alliance, which does not necessarily mean that they would be expected to despatch military forces outside their regions, or they might seek to retreat into neutralism or non-alignment. A third choice points towards some form of regionalism, whether it be the creation of new power blocs to rival the superpowers or the development of looser associations within each region, whose security would depend on the central strategic balance between the United States and the Soviet Union. A further development of this last pattern would be limited cooperation between these regional associations.

The annual summits of the industrialised states, underpinned by the concept of trilateralism, point in the first direction. Here is an embryonic global alliance. However, the severe economic conflicts among the partners are a serious if not insuperable obstacle in the way of a closer political association. There were signs of such coordination in the two or three summits following the Soviet invasion of Afghanistan, but recent indications of an American interest in resuming the dialogue with the Soviet Union, whatever the reasons, shifted the main focus of the London summit of 1984 back to the economic problems for which these meetings were established in the first place.[2] Moreover, constitutional and political reasons make it most unlikely that Japan would allow itself to be integrated into a formal alliance of this kind.

In each of the countries there are also popular currents which favour neutralist or non-aligned policies. Fed on anti-American sentiment and the fear of being dragged into a confrontation between the superpowers without being able to exercise control over their national destiny, such movements are a phenomenon of the political left and right. The Greens in Germany, Gaullists in France, the left of the Labour Party and nationalists of Enoch Powell's persuasion in Britain, the Japan Socialist Party and groups to the right within and outside the Liberal-Democratic Party, are all inclined in this direction. That does not mean that they share the same objectives. Some, especially those on the left, are looking for non-alignment on the Yugoslav or Swedish (during the Vietnam War) pattern and seek a link with those states of the Third World which pursue similar policies. Others, mainly on the right, dream of a militarily strong nation, able to defend its interests and extend its influence on the lines of traditional power politics as they have been conceived and practised in Europe for centuries.

In spite of tendencies towards the directions just described, it seems more likely that the third option will prevail and that in Europe and North-East Asia we will witness an increasing development of regionalism in one form or another. The dynamics of regionalism are most noticeable in Europe with the revival of interest in Western European Union (WEU), talk of turning the European Economic Community (EEC) into an effective instrument for the conduct of a European foreign policy, and the suggestion that this might hinge on the Paris-Bonn axis. But there are intimations of a similar trend in East Asia. The relationship between Japan and China is subtler than is indicated by talk of a Washington-Tokyo-Peking axis to block Soviet expansion, and both countries have shared intersts *vis-à-vis* the two great 'outsiders' in the region.

Regional associations, whatever form they might take, would increase the feeling of security against pressures from the Soviet Union and the uncertainties of American policies. They might also offer protection against the storms raging in the Third World. The International Energy Agency (IEA), though it includes the United States, Australia and New Zealand, is an example of the potential for inter-regional cooperation against the effects of those storms.[3]

TOWARDS REGIONALISM

The development of such associations raises two sets of basic questions. The first concerns their characteristics: what form would they take? How closely would they be integrated – a United States of Europe or a Sino-Japanese superstate? How would they be related to the United States? What weight would they have in world politics and would they seek to play a 'role' in the tradition of great powers?

The second series of questions is about the relations between the two groupings. Would they act independently of each other and be in competition or would they seek to cooperate? And if they follow the second course, would they coordinate their policies in order to strengthen their influence over the superpowers and in the rest of the world?

The factors driving Western Europe and Japan towards a greater regional integration are fairly obvious, though for historical reasons they are more visible in Europe than in East Asia. Since the end of the 1940s, the states of Europe have fallen quite neatly into three categories: those allied to the United States; those allied to the Soviet Union; and a few that are neutral or non-aligned.

The political structure of post-war Europe has become institutionalised through the settlement of West Germany's relations with the Soviet Union, Poland and Czechoslovakia; the inter-allied and inter-German agreements over Berlin; the Final Act of the Conference on Security and Cooperation in Europe (CSCE), on 1 August 1975; and the apparently interminable arms control negotiations in which the neutral/non-aligned states play a useful part by providing suitable meeting places.

There seemed to be a parallel development in East Asia in the late

1940s, especially after the communist victory in China. However, the confrontation between blocs, with no significant neutral states in between, came to an end with the inauguration of Kissinger's balance of power diplomacy at the beginning of the 1970s. It might have come sooner had it not been for American involvement in Vietnam, which prolonged the semblance of bloc confrontation in spite of the open hostilities between China and Russia.

In the decade that has passed, the situation in East Asia has become much more confused with a criss-cross pattern of conflicting and converging interests affecting all the four major powers in the region.

Embedded in a multilateral alliance with the United States, the West European states have almost from the beginning, and certainly since the issue of tactical nuclear weapons first appeared in the early 1950s, been haunted by two contradictory fears: that the United States might abandon them through some global arrangement with the Soviet Union or through a retreat into isolation and, on the other hand, that it might drag them into a devastating war in Europe.

These fears provided the impulse for policies seeking greater autonomy within the alliance. In addition, each of the major European countries tried to exploit the relationship with America for its own ends – the British using the 'special relationship' to mitigate their continental commitment; the French using the American shield in Germany to strengthen their independent 'role' in world affairs; the Germans using the American connection to strengthen their position in the Western alliance and as a base for their *Ostpolitik*.[4]

For Japan the situation was very different. Locked into a bilateral treaty, it has passed through various stages in its relationship with the United States, from occupation to partnership. In each phase it occupied a subordinate position and did not have the room for manoeuvre to exercise a greater independence in its foreign policy, which membership of a multilateral alliance might have afforded.

There can be no doubt that a desire for such independence existed from the beginning, even before the ending of the occupation.[5] The 1970s have marked the latest stage in this bilateral relationship. While not an equal of the United States in the political and military sense, the changing international environment, Japan's economic strength, and a recovered national self-confidence have encouraged Japanese leaders to think and talk in terms of playing an active part in world affairs.

There is much discussion today in Europe and Japan about the need to develop more independent orientations while retaining a basic security relationship with the United States. There is, however, an interesting contrast in the psychological context of these debates. All the major states of Western Europe – and a few minor ones as well – have an imperial past and were accustomed to regarding themselves as powers with global interests.

Britain and France, but not Germany, carried this outlook into the post-war period and took a long time to divest themselves of the idea that they were great powers of world-wide importance, alongside the

United States. Their membership of the victorious alliance, the possession of extensive overseas empires, and their acquisition of nuclear weapons gave some substance to this outlook. No one would argue today in support of such a position. Instead, Europeans have turned inwards and one detects a distinct flavour of parochialism in their attitudes. The Euro-centrism which in the past regarded the rest of the world as a playground for European politics has now become an almost exclusive preoccupation with Europe itself and its hinterlands in the Middle East and Africa. This is particularly noticeable in the public discussion of security problems, which is focussed on the North Atlantic region and, of course, Central Europe with its Scandinavian and Mediterranean flanks.

In Japan we can see the phenomenon in reverse. Following its defeat and surrender, it went into an enforced seclusion and became an appendage of American policy in the early post-war years. When it re-emerged in the 1960s as a result of its extraordinary economic growth, its governments tried to minimise the political impact of Japanese economic expansion, especially after the uproar in 1960 over the revision of the Mutual Security Treaty with the United States. On issues of international politics, especially in the United Nations, Japan continued to support the American position, albeit in a low key and with some nuanced reservations.

The American *rapprochement* with China and the impact of the first oil crisis in 1973-74 forced Japan into the open and launched a major debate over the direction of its policy. Still strongly committed to the bilateral relationship with the United States, Japan is now canvassing complementary arrangements, whether they be a special relationship with the Association of South-East Asian Nations (ASEAN),[6] closer ties with China, membership of wider 'Western Alliance',[7] or the creation of an Asia/Pacific Community.[8] For the time being these explorations are tentative and seen largely as a reinforcement of the Japanese-American alliance and not as a contradiction of it. However, in the future such initiatives may become more determined and will be seen as alternatives to the present security arrangements, should American protection cease to be credible or desirable or be withdrawn.

INTRA-REGIONAL COOPERATION

In both regions there is some movement away from the attitude which recognised the United States as undisputed leader of the alliances. While accepting the continued need for these treaties the West European nations and Japan claim an equal status with the United States in so far as the affairs of their own regions are concerned. In this they are not in conflict with American objectives. On the contrary, the American Government is encouraging a greater regional self-reliance which would enable it to devote more attention and resources to other areas threatened by the advance of Soviet power and influence.

What is more doubtful is whether there will be the same coincidence of interests in the long term over still more recent developments within the two regions. These changes include the search for regional autonomy from both superpowers and a tendency towards cooperation with states outside the Western alliance systems in pursuit of this aim.

The indications of a trend in that direction are as yet slight and might prove to be passing phenomena, caused by the strained relationship between the superpowers, and might fade away once the Soviet-American dialogue resumes and there is some relaxation of tension. Nevertheless, West European links with some of the East European states and the spreading contacts between Japan and China, strengthened by underlying economic interests, suggest that the two regions might become bridging zones in which governments coordinate their policies for the purpose of restraining the superpowers and mediating between them.

Such activities need not imply the dissolution of the alliance structures in Europe. Indeed, that would be most unlikely, given the Russian perception of the Warsaw Pact as a defensive glacis, essential for the security of the Soviet Union. The record of Soviet armed intervention in Hungary (1956) and Czechoslovakia (1968) reveals no tolerance of any hint that a member of the Warsaw Pact might wish to move into a neutral or non-aligned position.

Rumania's 'independence' has been tolerated because it has given no indication that it intends to leave the Pact, because of its ideological rectitude, and because its waywardness poses no serious geo-strategic threat to the Soviet Union. On the other hand, the Russians are very nervous over the development of relations between the two German Governments which might threaten their forward position in Europe.

The dismantling of the European blocs would be regarded by both superpowers and the European states as a dangerous and destabilising course, creating a vacuum which one or other of the superpowers might be tempted to fill, thus threatening to upset the global strategic balance between them. In East Asia the danger would be of a different kind. Instead of stopping short at a concerting of policies, China and Japan might eventually form a solid alliance which could become the most formidable combination in the world, challenging the United States and the Soviet Union in their tacit claim to joint global hegemony.

The creation of an East Asian superpower is still a remote possibility, much as the idea might appeal to some romantics in both countries. Even the establishment of a loose Sino-Japanese association, without entering into a formal alliance, would face formidable obstacles. The relations between Japan and China are a curious mixture of attraction and repulsion, which can be summarised in the following matrix:

ATTRACTION/REPULSION MATRIX OF SINO-JAPANESE RELATIONS

Attraction	Repulsion
Economic Complementarity –	Disappointed Economic Expectation:

Bilateral Factors	Japan's capital, technology, managerial skills & China's natural resources and huge market.	(Japan);[9] Fear of Economic Domination (China)
	Shared Culture (especially strong in Japan).	Touchiness over the other Party's Claim to 'Superiority'.[10]
	Geographical Proximity.	Territorial Disputes – Senkaku Islands;[11] conflicting claims over right to exploit resources in the East China Sea.
		Memories of War – Fear of Revival of Militarism (China).
International Environment	Common Front against 'Outsiders' & Unwillingness to be dragged into Conflicts beyond the Region.	Fear of Chinese or Japanese Domination of the Region.
	Search for Security against: Russian Expansion (China & Japan); Sino-Soviet *Rapprochement* (Japan); Japanese-Soviet *Rapprochement* (China); Sino-US *Rapprochement* (Japan); Economic Competition from US & EEC in China Market (Japan); US-Soviet *Rapprochement* (China & Japan).	Clash of Interests on Periphery of Sino-Japanese Zone: ASEAN/Indochina;[12] Siberian Development.[13]

Note: the names in brackets indicate that a particular attitude is especially strong in the country(ies).

For almost every factor pointing towards a convergence of Japanese and Chinese interests, there is another factor which makes for discord and conflict. The extent to which one or the other set of factors prevails will depend of course on how each government assesses the importance of their mutual relationship; an assessment subject to the pressures of domestic politics, perceptions of national interest, and the impact of the international environment.

Quite apart from the delicate balance of positive and negative features in the Sino-Japanese relationship, there is also a nagging uncertainty on the Japanese side over the future course of Chinese politics, particularly in the light of their many twists and turns since 1949. This is bound to impart great caution to Japanese dealings with China, lest Japan finds itself sucked into the orbit of its giant neighbour and becomes tied to its policies.

The evidence, therefore, suggests that, at best, progress towards regional integration in Europe and North-East Asia is likely to be slow and uneven. Nonetheless, there are also indications that the process is under way, more clearly across the ideological divide in Asia than in

Europe. The difference may be partly due to the fact that ideological divisions have never been so clear-cut in Asia.

There is, of course, a fundamental opposition between communism and a capitalism which is based on the operations of the market economy. But when one looks at the unmistakably Confucian aspects of the societies of North and South Korea or the flexible pragmatism of Chinese policies and the group orientation of Japanese society, in contrast to Western-style individualism, one wonders whether in Asia cultural traditions are not much more important than the clash of political philosophies.

The pace of regional integration may also differ because the United States and the Soviet Union are regarded to some extent as 'outsiders' in East Asia, whereas historically, culturally and by virtue of the post-war settlement, their presence in Europe is accepted as legitimate.

Nevertheless, there have been some interesting demonstrations that West and East European states may want to work together in a common cause. The case of the two German states is the most obvious example, though the planned summit between Chancellor Kohl and Chairman Honecker was obstructed by the Soviet Union.[14]

The Federal German Republic and the German Democratic Republic have much business which concerns themselves alone, but the deployment of Pershing II missiles in West Germany and the introduction of new Soviet missiles in East Germany have created a bond of unease between the two over relations with their respective 'protecting' powers. The Federal Government faces a strong opposition with neutralist overtones and must show that it is not surrendering control to Washington or Brussels over decisions affecting Germany. The East German régime has an analogous problem. Its opposition is more subdued but nonetheless real and is centred in the strong Federation of Protestant Churches, which are becoming a source of attraction for young people seeking alternative values to those of the state-imposed ideology. Such opposition in a totalitarian system is all the more dangerous since it threatens the legitimacy of the government and the state.

The evolution of Hungary's position in the European dialogue is another sign of the trend towards intra-European cooperation. Not only have the Hungarians come to the defence of the East-West German dialogue against Russian criticisms, but they also received Mrs Thatcher in February 1984 on her first visit to a Soviet Bloc country and prepared for similar visits from the West German Chancellor and the Italian Prime Minister. The longer established independent policies of Rumania and some of the smaller members of the Atlantic Alliance, often in contradiction of those of the alliance leaders, are a further illustration of this tendency.

The significance of the trend towards cooperation with countries outside the bounds of the alliance system in Asia has a different dimension since China formally ended its ties with the Soviet Union by not renewing their thirty-year-old Treaty of Friendship, Alliance and Mutual Assistance in April 1980. Sino-Japanese political cooperation has been most noticeable over Korea, especially in moves which might lead to the stabilisation of the situation on the lines of a 'German solution'. Both countries have unofficial and discreet relations with the Korean state in the hostile camp.[15] While Japan has used its economic strength to press China to restrain Kim Il-sung, it has also tried to exploit its economic power, so far unsuccessfully, to insert itself as mediator between Vietnam and ASEAN, especially by dangling the bait of economic aid to Vietnam. However, in South-East Asia, the Japanese adopt a more flexible position than the Chinese.

The member states of ASEAN established their association to promote a Zone of Peace, Freedom and Neutrality (ZOPFAN), though some of them are formally allied with Western powers. They have been blown off course in pursuit of this objective by their quarrel with Vietnam over Kampuchea, but they may well return to it once the Kampuchean issue is settled, especially as a number of the states, taking a long view, are even more fearful of China than of Vietnam. All this will present a conundrum to Japan in the future and may force its policymakers to make difficult choices which they would prefer to avoid.

The long-term aim of China and Japan is to reduce the impact of superpower rivalry on the region, but for the time being they are agreed that the danger stems primarily from the Soviet Union because of its greatly increased naval and air presence and its close association with Vietnam. Should the United States resume a more interventionist policy in East Asia, on the lines of its past involvement in Korea and Indochina, they would no doubt attempt to restrain it as well. Once the influence of both superpowers has declined or, at least, been kept at bay, we shall see whether Japan and China will clash over hegemony in Korea and South-East Asia or whether they will settle down to a joint management of the region.

COOPERATION BETWEEN THE REGIONS

The prospect for inter-regional cooperation is going to be determined by the speed and extent of West European political integration (how quickly will the appropriate machinery be in place and functioning, and will it include all the members of the European Communities or only some of them, clustered around a Paris-Bonn axis?); the extent of Sino-Japanese cooperation; the relations of Western Europe and Japan with the United States; and the course and impact of Soviet-American relations (would a renewed *détente*, for instance, slacken the momentum of intra-regional and inter-regional cooperation or accelerate it?).

However, assuming that the logic of events points to cooperation between Western Europe and Japan, because of shared interests in their dealings with the superpowers and the Third World, the success of such collaboration will depend ultimately on their willingness and ability to overcome the obstacles in its way. These obstacles exist on both sides,[16] but the more serious ones are to be found in Europe.

Japan is at a turning-point in its post-war history. Quite apart from American pressures to make it play a more active part in regional defence and in diplomatic and economic support of the West, it has its own reasons for not remaining over-reliant on the American connection for its security. A turn towards isolation, which has precedents in its history, is not seen to be the answer in an interdependent world where Japan's economic interests extend to every country. Instead, it is the fear of being isolated which accounts for the strong emphasis on the alliance with the United States while Japan cautiously explores the development of other international associations, all of which, with the exception of an association with China, are broadly within the Western camp.

Collaboration with Western Europe is one such option. So far it has been pursued within the context of the trilateral partnership of Europe, North America and Japan. The distinctive position of Western Europe and Japan, sandwiched between the superpowers, creates interests between them which are not identical with those of the United States and may on occasion be in conflict with them. European and Japanese cooperation over the Iran hostage crisis of 1979/80, their disagreement with the United States over sanctions against the Soviet Union, in particular over participation in the Siberian gas pipeline project, their unease over American policy in Central America, their opposition to some American economic policies, such as the running up of a huge budget deficit and the imposition of high interest rates, and their shared concern to promote an East-West dialogue, point to the value of Euro-Japanese cooperation. It would increase their autonomy in world affairs, would lighten Japan's heavy dependence on the United States, and would strengthen Japanese and European bargaining power in Washington and Moscow.

It is not surprising that the idea of collaboration has attracted more interest in Japan than in Europe. In the few practical examples of this tendency it is the Japanese who have taken the initiative, notably over the handling of the hostage crisis; Japan is, after all, a single state whereas on the European side there will be twelve (when Spain and Portugal join the Community in January 1986), all ready to argue among themselves over a common European foreign policy amid a welter of conflicting and disparate interests. But there are also more deep-seated difficulties.

Suggestions of a more systematic Euro-Japanese collaboration are received with incredulity in Europe and usually dismissed out of hand. Apart from a small minority of officials, business people, journalists, academics and others who have personal associations with Japan and Japanese people, most opinion formers and the general public view Japan with an indifference bordering on hostility. Indifference is an apt description of the state of the public mind in West Germany.

In Britain and France there also exists a good deal of partly submerged antipathy, for the word 'Japan' immediately conjures up the vision of a damaging trade competitor, which is reinforced by stereotypes of the wartime past. It seems to make little difference that the public often prefers Japanese goods to indigenous products. In the face of mass unemployment and shrinking world markets, Japan is a convenient scapegoat for rising protectionist and nationalist sentiment. The Japanese have contributed to this bad feeling by their slow and reluctant response to complaints over the protectionism in their own economy. In this respect there has been at least some progress though not sufficiently rapid to satisfy Japan's European and American trading partners. More serious in the long term is the change in Japanese attitudes which sometimes border on arrogance.

It is understandable that, after decades of modesty arising from shame over the past and post-war subordination to the United States, Japan should become more assertive as a result of its outstanding economic success and the feeling that after forty years the misdeeds of the past have been expiated. This trend is reinforced by the emergence of a generation which regards the war as history for which it cannot be expected to take responsibility. This change in mood is accompanied by growing irritation at criticisms of Japan from outside, and persuasive voices are being raised which call for a reassessment of the past, that borders on an apologia for the militarist phase in Japan's history.[17]

The main obstacle on the Japanese side to systematic collaboration with Europe is Japan's primary economic interest in the East Asia/Pacific region as a source of many essential raw materials except crude petroleum, the bulk of which is still imported from the Persian Gulf, and as a field for investment. It is economically the fastest growing area in the world with a huge potential for further development as a market for Japanese goods and services. It is the meeting place of the four most important stages of the twenty-first-century. Ironically, therefore, while Japan appears to be somewhat more receptive of the idea of Euro-Japanese cooperation than Europe, were one to take a long view it is the Europeans who should be paying more attention to such collaboration if they do not wish to live on the periphery of major developments in the future. Articles are already appearing in the British press lamenting a shift of American interest to the Pacific region, but they are couched in exclusively Eurocentric terms without any indication that the writers recognise the need for Europeans to become more interested in that part of the world.

Beneath the superpower stalemate, with its alternating periods of tension and *détente*, we may see a pattern of increasingly diverse relationships developing within the two regions at either end of the Eurasian landmass. There is a long way to go before one can envisage the establishment of bridging zones between East and West, with the two German states as the core in Europe and a Sino-Japanese association as the core in East Asia, but at least Western Europe and Japan share an interest in mitigating the effect of superpower rivalries. They might work fruitfully together in pursuit of this objective, if only because the outbreak of hostilities between East and West in one region may well spread to the other.

NOTES

1. Wolf Mendl, *Western Europe and Japan between the Superpowers* (London & Sydney, Croom Helm; New York, St. Martin's Press, 1984).
2. Although Prime Minister Nakasone was reported to have emphasised the political aspect of the summit (*The Japan Times Weekly*, 23 June 1984), the text of the final communiqué included an Economic Declaration and three short Statements dealing respectively with East-West Relations and Arms Control, International Terrorism, and the Gulf War. The Economic Declaration began by reaffirming that: 'The primary purpose of these meeting is to enable Heads of State or Government to come together to discuss economic problems, prospects and opportunities for our countries and the world'. (*The Times*, 11 June 1984).
3. The International Energy Agency, an association of oil-consuming countries, was set up in Paris on 15 November 1974, under the auspices of the Organisatien for Economic Cooperation and Development (OECD), in order to develop machinery and procedures to deal with the kind of supply crisis which occurred as a result of the Arab-Israeli war in October 1973.
4. Mendl, op. cit., pp.56-61.
5. This is particularly noticeable in the attempt by Japan to develop its own policy towards China, which caused difficulties with the United States in the negotiations leading to the San Francisco Peace Treaty of 1951. See Wolf Mendl, *Issues in Japan's China Policy* (London, Macmillan for The Royal Institute of International Affairs, 1978), pp.7-14.
6. Prime Minister Fukuda was the first to enunciate a clear line of policy towards ASEAN. See the text of his speech following his participation in the ASEAN summit at Kuala Lumpur in 1977. This became known as the 'Fukuda Doctrine' (*The Japan Times*, 19 August 1977).
7. This has been stressed most by Mr. Nakasone. In the list of Japanese policy choices, which he outlined in the Alastair Buchan Memorial Lecture to the International Institute for Strategic Studies, of 11 June 1984, cooperation with the West took first place: 'First Japan chooses as national policy to maintain our peaceful and stable society on the basis of political and economic cooperation and solidarity among the countries of North America, Western Europe and Japan – countries that share common values of freedom and democracy'. *Japan*, (London, Embassy of Japan Information Centre), No. 279, 21 June 1984.
8. Under Prime Minister Ohira, the government launched the idea of a Pan-Pacific Community as its guiding concept (*The Japan Times Weekly*, 14 July 1979).
9. See Wolf Mendl, 'Japan-China: the economic nexus', in Nobutoshi Akao, ed., *Japan's Economic Security: Resources as a Factor in Foreign Policy* (Aldershot, Gower for the Royal Institute of International Affairs, 1983), pp.223-28.
10. The uproar in 1982 over the revision of Japanese history textbooks is a recent example of this touchiness. The Chinese, and other Asians, feared that the suggested changes were an attempt to justify the claims to leadership in Asia which underlay Japan's military expansion in the past. On the other hand, the Japanese bridled at what they considered to be foreign interference in their domestic affairs and the Educational Affairs Division of the LDP, meeting in emergency session on 4 August 1982, urged the government not to yield to foreign pressure on this issue. (*The Japan Times Weekly*, 7 August 1982).
11. See Mendl, *Issues in Japan's China Policy*, pp.88-91.
12. Responding to pressure from ASEAN, Japan tries to keep a 'prudent balance' between its official aid to China and ASEAN. *The Straits Times*, 7 June 1982; *The Japan Times Weekly*, 17 March 1984.
13. Japan's decision not to participate in the construction of an oil pipeline associated with the second Siberian railway – the Baikal-Amur Mainline (BAM) – in 1974, can be attributed to Chinese concern over its strategic implications. See Gerald Curtis, 'The Tyumen Oil Development Project and Japanese Foreign Policy Decision-making', in Robert A. Scalapino, ed., *The Foreign Policy of Japan* (Berkeley, University of California Press, 1977).
14. *The Guardian*, 28, 30 & 31 July 1984; *The Times*, 3 August 1984.
15. For instances of Chinese contacts with South Korea and Japanese contacts with North Korea, facilitated respectively by Japan and China, see *The Japan Times Weekly*, 24 March 1984; *The Guardian*, 7 & 8 June 1984.
16. For a discussion of Euro-Japanese relations, see Reinhard Drifte, 'The European Community and Japan: Beyond the Economic Dimension' (*Journal of International Affairs*, Vol. 37 No. 1, Summer 1983, pp.147-63).
17. See, for example, *Japan Echo*, Special Issue on 'The War and Japan: Revisionist Views', Vol. XI, 1984, especially the articles by Irie Takanori, Kobori Keiichiro, Murakami Hyoe, Takeyama Michio.

PART IV:
Conclusions

8
Euro-Japanese Relations: Realities and Prospects

REINHARD DRIFTE

The first common theme of several contributors is the economic impact of Japan upon Western Europe. This impact appears almost intolerable in a number of European states where Japan's economic success is seen as a threat to vital sectors of industry, not only in their home markets but also in important third markets. This situation has produced numerous important consequences ranging from high unemployment to some questioning of the basic organisation of West European societies.

Several authors also mention that this important Euro-Japanese economic relationship is not paralleled by close political ties such as those which exist between Japan and the United States. However, similarities in the interests and international status of Western Europe and Japan suggest that mutual benefits could accrue from the fostering of stronger political links.

Europe's economic and political survival also depend upon the actions of its major partners – the United States and Japan – in the Asian region. For example the United States now conducts more of its trade with the Pacific region than with Western Europe. In broad terms East Asia is of growing economic, political and military importance; and the military alliance between Japan and American has been strengthened so that it is now far more effective than ever before. Due to America's increasing stake in the East Asian region there is now an element of competition between Western Europe and Japan in their relations with the United States.

Finally, it should be noted that Japan has consistently tried to carve out an economic zone in Asia whereas Europe has only recently begun to renew its interest in Asia, after decolonisation. The question may therefore arise as to whether Japan will pursue a special relationship with ASEAN, China or the USSR at the political, economic or even military expense of Europe.

This conclusion aims to place the theme of Euro-Japanese relations in a broad perspective, and to discuss important issues which have not been covered by other contributors or which deserve more detailed attention. The non-trade dimension of Euro-Japanese relations requires further discussion as too much comment tends to focus on commercial issues. I believe that frictions arising from trade cannot be approached creatively if other dimensions of the relationship are not given adequate consideration.

Since the late 1970s Western Europe's relations with Japan have attracted increasing public attention. This interest has been largely stimulated by the worsening trade imbalance not only between Japan and Western Europe but also between Japan and her other major trading partners. Faced with Japan's formidable economic challenge, which has produced higher unemployment and lost markets, Europeans are trying to understand its origins and how they should react to it.

The first European book on this issue was Hakan Hedberg's *The Japanese Challenge* which as early as 1970 shocked Europeans by describing Japan's economic progress, and predicting its impressive economic future. However, at that time, Europe still enjoyed a trade surplus with Japan and the main commercial issue was Japan's textile exports to Western Europe. Today books on Japan's economy are far more specific and focus on particular industrial sectors – such as automobiles – or Japanese personnel management.

The Japanese are themselves faced by a different challenge; namely how to live with the international repercussions of their economic success. In many fields of industry they have overtaken their former teachers, who were often Europeans. As a result they are confronted by resentment among their trading partners. In his chapter Yoshimori Masaru draws a parallel between British condemnation of Germany eighty years ago, and Western European criticism of Japan today. Like earlier industrial latecomers, who were eager to catch-up, Japan is not welcomed by the established economic powers. Thus, like Imperial Germany, Japan feels she is blamed for being too industrious and successful. Tokyo also has to fear a possible outbreak of commercial protectionism which could well begin in the United States.

If Western Europe followed the protectionist path this would have equally serious consequences for Japan, as others would be likely to follow suit. Thus, trade frictions are related to the way Japan conducts its general relations with the outside world, and Japan has to recognise that at the level of foreign policy it suffers handicaps which make it difficult to deal with the political problems of trade. Japan's handicaps involve policies, institutions and attitudes which are relevant to her broad relationships with foreign states.

These considerations lead one to discuss the political dimension of Euro-Japanese relations which has increasingly become the focus of discussions between Tokyo and Brussels. This is partly the result of the EC's 1976 declaration that the trade conflict had become a political issue, but also because both parties are gradually discovering a wide range of shared non-economic interests. If Japan 'lost' Western Europe, in a political sense, she would be diplomatically isolated, and increasingly dependent on the United States. Therefore, in recent years Japan has repeatedly emphasised that it shares the fundamental values of the industrial democracies, and considers itself a member of the Western group of nations.

THE ECONOMIC DIMENSION
In the calendar year 1983 Japan's trade surplus reached $20.45 billion. Its surplus with the United States was a record $18.1 bn. and that with the European Community an unprecedented $10.4 bn. Although the EC's exports to Japan grew by 7.4 per cent in the same year, Japan's exports to Europe rose by 8.6 per cent. Unemployment in the EC has recently reached 12.2 million which is 10.9 per cent of the employed population.[1]

Europeans consider all these figures interlinked, and claim that high unemployment is the unacceptable consequence of the trade imbalance between Japan and Europe. Japan rejects this intepretation, although Japanese leaders have come to recognise the political significance of high levels of unemployment, particularly for European politicians who have to seek reelection. Now, even though Japan's trade surplus is almost static European unemployment continues to rise.

The member states of the European Community have reacted to the trade imbalance at several levels, sometimes with and sometimes without the cooperation of the European Commission. The most dramatic steps have been the agreements on so-called voluntary restraints between Japan and the Commission. Japan has agreed to these so as to prevent even more damaging unilateral steps by Europeans. The most important such agreement was concluded in February 1983. This set a ceiling for three years on exports of VTRs, television sets, television tubes, motor vehicles, fork lift trucks, quartz watches, light trucks, motor cycles, tape recorders and hi-fi equipment. Another restrictive European measure has been the doubling of the import tariff on digital audio discs for five years. This is legal under the GATT if it is accompanied by appropriate compensation.[2]

The official rationale for such measures is the protection of sectors of European industry until they are able to compete with Japan after rationalisation and restructuring. However, it is doubtful if European industry is using this breathing space effectively. In fact it may become a mere stop-gap measure to help politicians who have to win elections, rather than a means towards improved competitiveness.

The problem is that these recent agreements are unmistakably protectionist measures, which may, in turn, lead to the growth of worldwide protectionism. Thanks to the moderating influence of the European Commission and some member states, pressures to close the Common Market have been alleviated. In fact bilateral measures such as British, French and Italian limits on the import of Japanese cars have been far more severe. In this case the role of an intermediate bureaucracy – which is often criticised for diluting policies – has proved highly beneficial, and has contributed decisively to reducing tensions in world trade.[3]

Other European measures are linked to the complaint that the Japanese market is insufficiently open. The structural problem is that both Japan and Europe are basically exporting the same range of manufactured products; but while the EC imports large quantities of manufactures Japan only imports roughly half as many. In contrast Japan's main imports are raw materials. On the European side the Commission has begun various export promotion schemes. These include the mounting of conferences on promising sectors of the Japanese market. In addition the European Commission gives 22 scholarships each year to young European businessmen to obtain on-the-job training in Japanese companies following a year of intensive language study.

The European Commission has also pressed Japan to take further steps to open its home market. Consequently the Japanese have taken a series of measures to ease market access by removing some non-tariff barriers (the existence of which the Japanese Government first recognised in 1982) and tariffs. However, it will be some time before these measures have much impact on the trade balance. The most important point is for European businessmen to realise that the Japanese market is worth a special effort, and that far more is at stake than a market of 120 million Japanese. Certainly, it will take a long time to destroy the image of an inpenetrable Japanese market which originated from direct experience of Japanese protectionism in the 1950s and 1960s.

Other measures which are more relevant to solving fundamental issues than they are to correcting the trade imbalance, are the promotion of technological exchange, joint ventures and investment. Such moves have been supported by the European Commission since the late 1970s under the general title of 'industrial cooperation'. The most promising of these fields appears to be the promotion of technological cooperation.

In practice, however, there are a number of obstacles to such developments. Although it is obvious that Europe and Japan can learn from each other, and that enormously expensive R&D activity should not be duplicated, some people are cool towards joint activity. Indeed, some Europeans fear that technical cooperation could provide Japan with technology in those few industrial sectors where European companies still maintain an advantage.

Some countries consider that technological cooperation is not an appropriate matter to be handled by the Commission, or dealt with at the multilateral level. Since 1983 the EC Commission has proposed an agreement with Japan on scientific and technical cooperation, but the above mentioned reservations have prevented the endorsement of this idea by the Council of Ministers. Nevertheless, several bilateral schemes for technological and scientific cooperation do exist. In the meantime the Commission has begun to organise conferences between European and Japanese businessmen on aspects of technological cooperation. These take place alternately in Brussels and Tokyo. In January 1983 a pilot study commissioned by the EC Commission was published dealing with various aspects of this question.

Joint ventures are very often seen as panaceas for entering the Japanese market or securing Japanese technology. But experience has shown that Europeans need to handle such ventures with greater skill if the Japanese are not to be the sole beneficiaries. Some companies also see joint ventures as a substitute for generating their own forms of technological development.

Another problem related to joint ventures or Japanese investment in Europe is labour relations. In considering possible joint ventures in Europe, many Japanese companies are opposed to the so-called Vredeling proposal which would oblige their enterprises in Europe to disclose corporate information and consult employee representatives.

Another danger inherent in promoting Japanese investment in Europe is that of attempting to use such investment as a mere means towards balancing the trade figures. Indeed, instead of looking at the overall implications of Japanese investment some countries have sought to use it to solve their trade problems, and unemployment in their depressed regions. As the recent example of the Nissan car factory in Britain has shown some Japanse investment does not necessarily do much to relieve unemployment.

THE AMERICAN FACTOR

A very important element in the Euro-Japanese economic relationship is Japan's economic connection with the United States. For Japan her relationship with America is clearly more important than her links with Europe. This is the result of political and military as well as economic factors. However, the economic nexus is central and very influential. In Japanese-American relations it should also be remembered that the Japan-United States Security Treaty contains an economic element, which is in fact mentioned in the treaty itself. Furthermore the Japanese production of American weapons under licence has provided Japan with significant amounts of high technology.

The United States continues to be Japan's most important trading partner, with an annual total trade of over $60 billion. Until the late 1960s the United States allowed Japan almost unlimited access to her domestic market. America also did much to promote Japan's membership of international economic organisations such as GATT and the OECD. In contrast Europeans adopted rather a restrictive attitude on both issues. Today 58.9 per cent of Japan's foreign technology comes from the United States, compared to only 40.4 per cent from Europe.[6]

In general, Europe can do nothing but live with the practical consequences of this situation. Regarding the notion of Euro-Japanese joint ventures, many Japanese companies are more interested in such ventures with American partners and are more likely to invest in the United States which has some clear practical advantages over Europe. Indeed, in the period 1951-82 the grand total of Japan's direct investment in the United States was $14 bn. as compared with only $6.1 bn. in the whole of Europe.[7] Due to heavy American influence on Japanese policy makers Japan is likely to be much more responsive to American than EC demands. Since American and European demands on Japan are sometimes the same – for example on non-tariff barriers – American strength can be of help to Europe. On the other hand, when Euro-American cooperation has been too close, say, in urging Japan to open its market, it is perceived by Tokyo as an unpleasant 'ganging-up' against her. At the end of 1981 the United States proposed regular meetings between the highest level trade representatives of the EC, Canada, Japan and the United States. Since then these quadrilateral meetings have contributed to easing the problems which Brussels, Washington and Ottawa all have with Tokyo.

THE ROLE OF EUROPEAN ECONOMIC INTEGRATION
Finally, it is necessary to consider the impact of European economic integration on the Euro-Japanese economic relationship. On both economic and political levels the integration of the EC leaves much to be desired. Even between member states protectionism has become a serious problem, and the accession of Spain and Portugal to the Community will strain the European consensus even further.

In relations with Japan, as in relations with the United States it is obvious that a United Europe would have greater influence than a Europe in which national egoisms are dominant. It is the absence of a common industrial policy which prevents the European Community implementing a unified trade policy towards Japan. This lack has also prevented the conclusion of an EC-Japan trade agreement. According to the Treaty of Rome such an agreement should already have been concluded as the Commission is supposed to direct the Community's overall external trade.

Several member states are unwilling to surrender safeguard clauses in their bilateral trade agreements with Japan while Japan is unwilling to accept such safeguards in a new multilateral agreement. In the past such disunity has given Japan ample opportunity to play off one EC member state against another. However, since the beginning of the 1980s Japan has increasingly recognised the Commission as an interlocutor in trade negotiations, and realises the helpful role of the Commission as an intermediate bureaucracy. Of course, it is only greater cohesion in the Community which will permit the Commission to play more than this limited buffer role.

LEARNING FROM JAPAN
Another approach in reaching a more balanced economic relationship between Europe and Japan is attempting to learn from the Japanese economic experience. For several years a spate of books, conferences and lectures have advocated 'learning from Japan'. If something can be learnt from Japan this would certainly help to increase the competitiveness of European business and industry.

But when one examines the relevant literature in this field it is soon apparent that such a learning process cannot be limited to the simple transfer of personnel management methods or production technologies. When Japanese refer, for example, to the 'British disease' or classify some West European countries as 'former developed countries' they not only question Europe's industrial performance but also the organisation of European societies and value systems.

A series of books have appeared in the United States, and somewhat later, in Western Europe which attempt to explain Japan's economic success. This recent literature can be divided into two broad streams. One describes Japanese management methods and technology – along the lines of William G. Ouchi's *Theory Z* or Richard Tanner Pascale and Anthony G. Athos's *The Art of Japanese Management*. These books are extremely positive and emphasise the lessons which Western businesses could draw from Japan.

A second stream of books seeks to destroy the Japanese 'economic myth' and draws attention to the social costs of the Japanese experience – to prove the impossibility of learning positively from Japan. These authors also complain about the use of the Japanese model made by Europeans employers or conservative politicians to make their employees work harder, or to justify reductions in social benefits.

These critiques of the 'Japanese model' are certainly right to point out that the 'model' does not exist in the clearcut form presented in much of the 'learn from Japan' literature. Lifetime employment exists for only a small part of the Japanese labour force and compulsory retirement at 55 cannot be called 'lifetime' employment – particularly in a country which boasts one of the highest life expectancies in the world. Furthermore, the seniority system is increasingly being revised due to economic constraints.

In fact, structural differences between the economies of Western Europe and Japan alone place considerable limits on the transfer to Europe of many aspects of the Japanese 'model'. The major states of Europe do not have a dual economic structure and labour-employee relationships are organised differently from in Japan. Furthermore, it is wrong to praise Japan's employment system by comparing Japan's unemployment figures with those of Western Europe since the Japanese definition of unemployment is significantly narrower than that in Europe. Moreover, critiques of the 'Japanese model' are right to draw attention to the social costs of the Japanese system, such as the unequal development of private and public facilities (for example, the lack of parks) the underdeveloped social security system, and serious ecological problems.

All these issues should not prevent us from drawing some positive conclusions from the Japanese experience. The genre of literature which is content to destroy the 'myth' of the 'Japanese model' by showing only the negative aspects of the Japanese economic experience, or the 'impossibility' of transferring elements from it, merely encourages those who are always reluctant to learn from a non-European experience. This is both intellectually and economically suicidal. Furthermore it gives additional strength to those who advocate protectionism and isolation. Isolationists tend to argue that as the Japanese have a totally different economic and cultural system it is impossible to compete with them unless Europeans abandon their own way of life.

One instructive point for Europeans is the Japanese attitude to technology. Against a background of widespread cultural pessimism in Europe technology has come to be viewed as a curse of modern civilisation, more specifically, as a job killer. In contrast, Japanese tend to believe that technology can solve almost all today's problems. Closely connected with this attitude is the Japanese belief in progress. Examples of this include the recent World Technology Exhibition held in the science city of Tsukuba in 1985, and various government projections of future economic trends.

In addition, the Japanese experience technological innovation as a pleasure. The Japanese consumer is constantly encouraged to buy gadgets which are based on the most advanced technology; for example calculators or voice recognising machines in pocket format. Traditional products such as watches are also given a new attraction by incorporating into them TV sets with liquid crystal screens. It sometimes seems as though the whole society is engulfed in technological ecstasy.

It will certainly be difficult to transfer this enthusiasm for technology to Europe, but with their negative attitudes Europeans forego too many of the positive attributes of technology. What is more, Japan's enthusiasm for technology makes much economic sense. The use of new technology in mass consumer products reduces the cost of what are initially very expensive items such as ICs, and has given Japan a lead in other product lines, where a new technology can be used in a more economical way. One vivid example is numerically controlled machine tools where Japan has become a strong competitor of Western Europe.

This different Japanese attitude is also expressed in the better education and training of engineers. In 1982, 73,000 or 20 per cent of all Japanese university graduates received engineering degrees, 9,000 completed 5-year technical school courses, and tens of thousands were trained in vocational high schools. All these figures are much higher than in Europe or the United States.[9]

Another field where Europe can learn from Japan is the management of enterprises. Japanese factories run by Japanese in several European countries have proved that Japanese management methods are not so alien to Europeans that they cannot benefit from them. In particular, workers on the shop floor in Japanese-run factories in Britain and France enjoy a greater sense of equality which is the result of Japanese management methods. For example, there is a marked lack of social privileges for Japanese managers.[10] The basic concept of Japanese personnel management is to regard an enterprise as a community in which interdependence demands solidarity and involvement, and where the creativity of employees at all levels is tapped to the maximum. More specifically, Japanese-style Quality Control Circles are finding more and more adherents in European companies.

Thus 'Learning from Japan' does not imply the transfer of a mythical 'Japanese model' or the use of such a model for political purposes. In fact, research carried out by Michael White and Malcolm

Trevor established that Japanese-run factories in Britain had succeeded without introducing a lifetime employment system, a company union, seniority-based social benefits or a group decision-making processes involving British employees.[11]

Furthermore, 'learning from Japan' does not imply the mere transfer of techniques of management and production organisation, piecemeal, without enquiring into the local cultural background. Rather, it means a useful questioning of the enterprise's employer-employee relationship and of organisation production.

Thus, the Japanese experience can help Europeans to see their problems in a new light and use their stock of abilities and values more efficiently. One of the surprising results of White and Trevor's study is that there appears to be a 'fortunate correspondence between the requirements of the Japanese production system and some of the traditional values of the British working class'.[12] Putting these lessons into practice will not be easy since it involves the abandonment of well-established attitudes. Such lessons also have important political and social consequences – since Europeans would have to remove existing obstacles to social flexibility and the fostering of talent in their own societies.

THE POLITICAL DIMENSION

In the post-war years Europe and Japan have failed to develop a political relationship which matches their close economic links. In their contributions Gordon Daniels and Endymion Wilkinson trace the development of Euro-Japanese political relations and provide some explanation of this imbalance. They also discuss why the American-Japanese relationship is far stronger than that between Europe and Japan. In the following paragraphs I will discuss this problem against the background of the general difficulties which Japan encounters in establishing overseas relationships. I will also suggest some further explanations for the somewhat undeveloped character of Euro-Japanese political relations.

It is interesting to recall how the political dimension of Euro-Japanese relations became a public issue and how the public became aware of its existence. In October 1976 Euro-Japanese relations had reached a crisis point when a Keidanren delegation, led by Toshio Doko visited the European Community. At this time politicians in the EC thought that it would be profitable to discuss the 'politicisation' of relations between Europe and Japan. Largely as a result of the Japanese trade surplus with the EC of $3 bn.

European leaders said that relations with Japan had become a political issue. According to this analysis the growth of Japanese trade threatened European jobs which in turn affected European politics. It is clear that European leaders were using the term 'politicisation' as a tactical ploy to prompt the Japanese to moderate their trade offensive.[13] Despite some obvious common political interests there was still no obvious political dimension to Euro-Japanese relations. On the contrary, the trade problem tended to obstruct the development of a political relationship since both sides were too absorbed by it.

Since 1976 the political dimension of Euro-Japanese relations has become more apparent. Both sides have become increasingly aware of shared interests, and the value of obtaining the other's support on certain international issues. It is likely that the major impetus for this change came from the Japanese. Until the late 1970s Japan concentrated most of her attention on her economy, and thanks to American protection her foreign policy was chiefly concerned with trade.

In Japan's bilateral relations with other states, such as Communist China, she insisted in separating political and economic issues. However, the 1973 oil shock demonstrated that the United States was not always a reliable partner, and that there could be issues on which Japanese and American interests might clash. At the same time, the United States began to press Japan to accept a greater defence burden and become more active in foreign policy.

As a result, Tokyo began to embark upon a more independent diplomacy. In this setting an informal ally like Western Europe appeared extremely valuable. Japan realised that she had more in common with EC states than America in the Middle East. Furthermore, though both Japan and Europe are closely allied with the United States both share a desire to preserve their political independence *vis-à-vis* Washington.

As a result of Japan's new awareness of Europe's value high level political contacts gradually increased from the late 1970s. Furthermore, the subjects of these exchanges went well beyond trade issues. In March 1983 on the initiative of the Japanese Foreign Minister, the EC Foreign Ministers decided to hold consultations every six months between the Japanese Foreign Minister and the EC President. So far this is the highest level of political consultation which has been arranged, apart from bilateral consultations.

Yet despite this improvement and the broadening of political relations Euro-Japanese political cooperation is still hindered by many problems. One difficulty is Japan's sense that she is not considered a full member of the Western camp and that in time of crisis she may be left without help. For example, Japan felt humiliated when she was excluded from the Guadeloupe summit meeting in December 1978 – at the instigation of European leaders. In the following year an EC internal report on trade relations with Japan referred to the Japanese as 'workaholics living in rabbit hutches'. This did little to endear Europe to the Japanese.

Several factors may explain this situation. One is Europe's experience of Japan's former 'omnidirectional' or 'multidirectional' diplomacy. This aimed at friendship with everyone while at the same time avoiding a clear stance on international issues. American protection partly explains this Japanese stance but it also reflects Japan's profound feeling of vulnerability. Despite changes in Japanese foreign policy which have been induced by shifts in American diplomacy this feeling of vulnerability is likely to continue for some time. It is based upon Japan's dependence on imports for virtually all her raw materials, and her need for open export markets.

The EC also senses its international vulnerability but Japan's geographical and political isolation in East Asia has produced a much deeper sense of vulnerability in her outlook. In the past this outlook served to counter growing demands and accusations from abroad regarding Japan's passive diplomacy or aggressive trade policies. Japan will not easily abandon this 'cult of vulnerability' since it has proved so useful in both her domestic and foreign policies. This is evidenced by the following comment by a Japanese economist:[14]

> 'Japan will lose its ability to deal with crises and its cohesion if it loses its sense of vulnerability – which is why we continue harping on the subject of our reliance on outside sources of supply beyond our control. If we should rearm and become a world military power, we would . . . reduce our effectiveness and limit the ways in which the government can cynically manage business and manipulate national consensus'.

A recent example of Japan's sense of vulnerability is her position on the new Law of the Sea. Several industrialised powers such as the United States, Britain, France, and the Federal Republic of Germany have concluded an agreement on the exploitation of sea-bed resources but Japan did not adhere to it since she was worried about possible negative reactions in developing countries. However this did not prevent the Japanese Government passing a bill which makes later adherence to the agreement possible. This issue illustrates one limit to political cooperation between Europe and Japan.

Other limits to political cooperation are largely the result of differences of mutual perception. Most Europeans still consider Japan to be essentially different in culture, politics and economic organisation. The adverse impact of this attitude on economic relations has already been outlined.

Furthermore, the Japanese themselves encourage these European views by their obsession with their own 'uniqueness'. This thinking finds expression in the so-called *Nihonjinron*. This holds that Japan consists of a distinct, separate, unit of humanity which cannot be understood by outsiders. Therefore, Japanese tend to think that in the last analysis all their difficulties with foreign countries are based on 'misunderstandings'.

Needless to say, this is an extremely convenient explanation of disagreement which places most blame on the other side. Since the appearance of Endymion Wilkinson's book *Misunderstanding* its title has become a Japanese catchphrase. This trend is evident since the Japanese Foreign Ministry has distributed Wilkinson's book free of charge to European opinion leaders. This action ignores the fact that the book describes Japanese misunderstanding of Europe, as well as European misperception of Japan.

The Japanese obsession with their own uniqueness is not only harmful, it is mistaken. All human beings share the same range of values but people differ in the emphasis which they place on a particular value. For example, the desire for harmony is certainly not a uniquely Japanese concept. It is shared by all human beings. However the Japanese may emphasise harmony more than many other peoples. They are also willing to make greater sacrifices in order to achieve it. Sacrifices to achieve harmony can be very great, and in international relations may produce makeshift solutions, which are open to varying interpretations. These can, in turn, lead to misunderstanding and distrust.[15]

The concept of Japanese uniqueness is also harmful in international life as it implicitly rejects all attempts at mutual understanding. It also makes it difficult for foreigners to accept the Japanese Government's repeated assertion that Japan shares the same fundamental views as the West, and considers itself a member of the Western group of nations. Indeed, at the the policy level misperceptions also make it difficult to assess the policies of a partner or rival.

Japan is often dismissed as a political pygmy which is resigned to accepting orders from the United States – though this image is gradually fading. Gaullists in particular continue to have difficulty in accepting a country which relies so much on a superpower in such fields as defence, which are generally considered crucial to the safeguarding of national sovereignty. Very often Europeans are insufficiently informed about Japanese political conditions, or are over concerned with their own foreign policies.

A final, very important problem in Euro-Japanese relations is the lack of a coherent European foreign policy. This is a consequence of the incomplete process of European integration and is a significant obstacle to the development of Euro-Japanese political relations. Where interests coincide Japan would certainly support the European view more often – if only there was a coherent European voice. As Euro-Japanese political relations remain undeveloped their relations still lack a sophisticated institutional framework for specialist consultation and negotiation.

In short, only a Western Europe which speaks with one voice can bring a mature political dimension with relations with Japan. If both parties come to see their relations as of great political importance it will also be easier to find solutions to their trade problems. Even without a security treaty linking Japan and Europe mutual recognition of the political significance of their relations remains a practical and important goal.

NOTES

1. *Neue Zürcher Zeitung* 14/15 January 1984.
2. Agence Europe 25 March 1983 and 1 December 1983
3. The following draws heavily on my article 'The European Community and Japan, Beyond the Economic Dimension' in *The Journal of International Affairs* (New York) Vol. 37, No. 1. Summer 1983.
4. 'Prospects of Technology Transfer from Japan', Prepared by Japan Business Services, Tokyo, January 1983.

5. *Financial Times* 16 January 1984. *Neue Zürcher Zeitung* 25 October 1983.
6. Report on the Survey of Research and Development; Statistics, Bureau of the Prime Minister's Office, Tokyo, 1981.
7. (12-83-2) Foreign Press Centre, Japan June 1983.
8. Du-Yul Song *Ist Japan ein Modell für Deutschland?* East Asian Institute, Free University of Berlin, Berlin 1982, or Helmut Demes, *Ist das japanische Industrial Relations System (IRS) auf die BRD übertragbar?* East Asian Institute, Free University of Berlin, Berlin 1983. A very malicious work from this stream of literature is Ariane Dettloff and Hans Kirchmann, *Arbeitsstaat Japan. Exportdrohung gegen die Gewerkschaften*, Hamburg, Rowohlt, 1981.
9. *Japan Times Weekly* 5 March 1983.
10. Michael White and Malcolm Trevor, *Under Japanese Management* London, Heinemann 1983.
11. *Ibid* p.124.
12. *Ibid* p.134.
13. Drifte, see f.n.3.
14. *Far Eastern Economic Review* 12 June 1981.
15. *Asahi Evening News* 17 January 1982.

PART V
Data and Documents

JAPAN–EUROPE–USA
August 1945-December 1985

A Brief Chronology

1945

15 August Emperor of Japan accepts surrender demand issued by USA, Britain and China.

30 August General Douglas MacArthur arrives in Japan to take command of Occupation.

2 September Japanese Surrender signed on USS *Missouri*, Tokyo Bay. Signatories include USA, Britain, France, the Netherlands and USSR.

1946

19 January Supreme Commander for the Allied Powers, Douglas MacArthur, establishes International Military Tribunal for Far East. Judges include representatives from USA, Britain, France, the Netherlands and USSR.

8 February First units of British Commonwealth Occupation Force arrive in Japan.

5 April First Meeting in Tokyo of Allied Council for Japan. Consultative organ consisting of USA, USSR, China and British Commonwealth.

1947

February Beginning of withdrawal of sections of British Commonwealth Occupation Force – for economic reasons.

5 June US Secretary of State, Marshall, announces plan to aid European economic recovery.

15 August MacArthur permits beginning of Japanese private foreign trade.

1948

6 January US Secretary for the Army, Royall, states that Japan is barrier against Communism.

16 April Sixteen West European states sign European Economic Cooperation Agreement.

12 November International Military Tribunal for Far East issues its verdicts.

1949

1 April NATO treaty signed.

25 April Single exchange rate for Japanese Yen put into effect.

1 November US Department of State announces it is considering a Japanese Peace Treaty.

1950

6 January Cominform attacks moderation of Japan Communist Party.

25 June Outbreak of Korean War. British, Belgian, Dutch, French, Greek, Turkish and Luxembourg troops join largely American UN force.

14 September President Truman orders beginning of negotiations for Peace Treaty with Japan.

1951

20 June Japan affiliates to UNESCO and the ILO.

8 September Japanese Peace Treaty signed at San Francisco. Signatories include USA, Britain, France, Belgium, the Netherlands, Luxembourg, Norway and Greece.

8 September USA and Japan sign Security Treaty.

1952

28 April Japan's sovereignty restored. Occupation ends.

14 August Japan joins International Monetary Fund and International Bank for Reconstruction and Development.

22 October First British Nuclear Weapon Test.

1953

27 July Armistice in Korean War.

1 August Japan joins International Wheat Agreement.

24 December USA agrees to return the Amami Oshima islands to Japan.

1954

24 July Japan joins Economic Commission for Asia and the Far East (ECAFE).

5 October Japan participates in Consultative Committee of Colombo Plan.

23 October West Germany's sovereignty restored.

1955

1 June Beginning of Japanese-Soviet negotiations for restoration of relations after Second World War.

14 June German Federation of Industries calls for emergency safeguards against Japanese imports.

10 August Quorum filled for Japanese membership of GATT. Britain, France, Belgium and the Netherlands invoke article 35 withholding Most Favoured Nation treatment (MFN).

1956
May   West Germany liberalises 80% of bilateral imports from Japan – on MFN basis.

12 December   Japanese-Soviet diplomatic relations restored following Second World War.

18 December   Japan admitted to United Nations.

1957
25 March   EEC and Euratom Treaties signed at Rome.

April   Japan calls for general conference of GATT to discuss creation of EEC.

6 December   Japanese-Soviet commercial treaty signed.

1958
1 January   Inauguration of European Economic Community.

16 June   US-Japan Nuclear Power Agreement signed.

12 September   Japan and USA agree on revision of Security Treaty.

1959
August   During tour of Europe Prime Minister Kishi visits Bonn to request liberalisation of German trade policy.

26 Oct-20 Nov   GATT general meeting held in Tokyo.

20 November   European Free Trade Association (EFTA) agreement signed.

1960
April   Chancellor Adenauer visits Japan; favours liberalisation of imports from Japan.

23 June   Japan and USA sign new Security Treaty.

1 July   German-Japanese trade agreement signed. Japan granted full MFN treatment.

1961
July   Foreign Minister Kosaka visits Rome for trade liberalisation talks.

November   Japan says she will liberalise wide range of imports.

December   EEC Commissioner Rey visits Japan. Agreement to hold regular information meetings. Meetings never held.

1962
September   London *Economist* articles 'Consider Japan' highlight Japan's rapid economic progress.

November   Prime Minister Ikeda tours Europe to aid bilateral trade talks and Japan's application to join OECD.

14 November   Anglo-Japanese Commercial Treaty signed.

1963
March   Trade Protocol between Japan and Benelux states initialled. Japan granted MFN treatment.

14 May   New Franco-Japanese trade agreement signed; includes Safeguard Clause against rapid inrush of Japanese goods.

June   EEC Commission proposes common trade policy towards Japan.

1964
28 April   Japan joins OECD.

July   New German-Japanese trade protocol brings further liberalisation.

October   Tokyo Olympics.

1965
April   Japanese Foreign Ministry favours policy of export promotion in Europe.

June   Keidanren Mission visits EEC Commission; Europeans criticise 'subsidies' for Japanese shipbuilding.

September   Semi-annual consultations begin between European Coal and Steel Community and Japanese Ministry of Trade and Industry.

1966
21 January   Japan-Soviet Civil Aviation Agreement signed.

October   Japan requests negotiations with Europe on mutual trade liberalisation.

Japan's GNP overtakes that of Italy.

1967
May   German Foreign Minister Brandt visits Tokyo to discuss Nuclear Non-Proliferation Treaty.

1 July   European Communities (EC) formed from EEC, ECSC, and Euratom.

Japan's GNP overtakes that of Britain.

1968
1 July   Beginning of EC Customs Union.

November   Von Dohnanyi, Secretary of State of German Economics Ministry, visits Japan; praises Japanese planning and management.

Japan's GNP overtakes that of France.

1969
June   EC-Japan Textile Agreement – increases quotas of Japanese imports.

October   Britain proposes abolition of all restrictions on mutual trade with Japan.

Japan's GNP overtakes that of West Germany.

1970
2 February   European Parliament debates relations with Japan for first time.

20 July   EC Commission mandated to conduct negotiations for EC trade agreement with Japan.

November   EC Commissioner Dahrendorf visits Japan for talks on EC-Japan Trade

Treaty. EC demand for Safeguard Clause prevents agreement.

1971
March EC Commissioner Dahrendorf warns European Parliament that 'emotional criticism' of Japanese economic behaviour will soon be outdated.

6-8 July EC-Japan trade agreement talks again end in deadlock on Safeguard Clause issue.

27 September Emperor and Empress of Japan tour Western Europe; encounter anti-Japanese demonstrations in the Netherlands.

1972
February Prime Minister Sato proposes regular ministerial consultations with EC Commission.

May EC Commissioner Dahrendorf visits Japan for trade agreement talks. No agreement.

2 October Japan Foundation created to promote Japanese cultural exchange programmes.

1973
4 May Foreign Minister Ohira visits Brussels and agreess with EC Commission that regular consultative talks should be held.

June First high-level official consultations between EC and Japan.

26 Sept-10 Oct Prime Minister Tanaka visits, Paris, Bonn, London and Moscow to discuss EC-Japan relations and economic cooperation.

1974
9 February EC Commission refuses to extend Italy's quota restriction on Japanese tape-recorders.

18-23 February President of EC Commission Ortoli visits Japan and stresses need to strengthen relations.

October British Society of Motor Manufacturers and Traders (SMMT) calls for EC-wide quota on Japanese car imports.

1975
21 October Formal opening of EC Delegation in Tokyo.

15-17 November Prime Minister Miki attends Summit of Seven Advanced Industrial Nations at Rambouillet, France.

11-12 December Japan-EC Textile Agreement – including Japanese Voluntary Self Restraints, Japan to phase out textile restrictions on EC goods.

1976
10 March EC Commissioneer Sir Christopher Soames calls Japanese cars the main issue in Euro-Japanese relations.

27-28 June Prime Minister Miki attends Summit of Seven Advanced Industrial Nations, Puerto Rico, USA.

15-31 October Keidanren mission, led by Mr Doko, tours Western Europe. Subject to bitter criticism over Japan's Trade surplus (the 'Doko Shock').

1977
5 February EC Commission announces imposition of 20% anti-dumping duty on Japanese ball-bearing imports. (Later declared illegal by European Court.)

6-8 May Prime Minister Fukuda attends Summit of Seven Advanced Industrial Nations, London.

11 October EC Commission President Roy Jenkins visits Japan to 'consolidate political relationship.'

1978
30 January EC Commission President Roy Jenkins suggests Japan buys 20 Airbuses as a 'symbolic gesture.'

1 April Japan allows foreign car companies three years to adapt to Japan's severe emission standards.

16-17 July Prime Minister Fukuda attends Summit of Seven Advanced Industrial Nations, Bonn.

1979
30 March British newspapers publish confidential EC report which refers to Japanese as 'workaholics' and their houses as 'little more than rabbit hutches.'

28-29 June Summit of Seven Advanced Industrial Nations in Tokyo.

October EC issues plan for 22 annual scholarships for young executives to train in Japan (ETP).

1980
19 April Japan announces US$100m aid to Turkey.

22-23 June Foreign Minister Okita attends Summit of Seven Advanced Industrial Nations in Venice.

17 November Foreign Minister Ito calls for broader political and economic relations with Europe.

1981
9-21 June Prime Minister Suzuki tours West Germany, Italy, Belgium, England, the Netherlands and France; visits EC Commission.

20-21 July Prime Minister Suzuki attends Summit of Seven Advanced Industrial Nations, Ottawa.

2 September US proposes trilateral trade talks with Japan and EC. Japan agrees.

1982
30 January Japanese Government decides to

establish Trade Ombudsman to deal with foreign complaints regarding the opening of Japanese market.

4-6 June Prime Minister Nakasone attends Summit of Seven Advanced Industrial Nations, Versailles.

16 November USSR deploys MIG 21s on Etorofu, one of four islands north of Hokkaido claimed by Japan.

1983
12 February Japan and EC agree to 3-year restraint on Japanese VTR exports to EC.

11 March Companies from Japan, USA, UK and West Germany agree to cooperate in developing new jet engine.

28-30 May Prime Minister Nakasone attends Summit of Seven Industrialised Nations, Williamsburg, USA.

1984
9-12 May President of EC Commission Gaston Thorn visits Japan.

15 May First Japan-EC Ministerial Conference; Japan-EC Trade Expansion Committee established on an experimental basis.

8-9 June Prime Minister Nakasone attends Summit of Seven Advanced Industrial Nations, London.

1985
9 April Japan announce new market opening measures.

2-4 May Prime Minister Nakasone attends Summit of Seven Advanced Industrial Nations, Bonn.

12-20 July Prime Minister Nakasone visits Italy, France and EC Commission.

TABLE 1
EC/Japan bilateral trade (Eurostat), customs clearance, exports FOB, imports CIF (1973-83).

Million US$

Year	Imports from Japan		Exports to Japan		Balance	Cover ratio
	Mio $	Annual % Increase	Mio $	Annual % Increase	Mio $	%
1973	4.427	+ 40	2.856	+69	− 1.571	65
1974	5.461	+ 23	3.334	+ 17	− 2.127	61
1975	6.433	+ 18	2.800	− 16	− 3.633	44
1976	7.892	+ 23	3.067	+ 10	− 4.825	39
1977	9.786	+ 24	3.551	+ 16	− 6.235	36
1978	12.099	+ 24	4.783	+ 35	− 7.316	40
1979	14.185	+ 17	6.390	+ 34	− 7.795	45
1980	18.526	+ 31	6.387	± 0	− 12.139	34
1981	18.091	− 2	6.257	− 2	− 11.834	35
1982	17.587	− 3	6.180	− 1	− 11.407	35
1983	18.285	+ 4	6.489	+ 5	− 11.786	35

Table 2
EC/Japan bilateral trade (Ministry of Finance, Japan) customs clearance, exports FOB, imports CIF (1973-83).

Million US$

Year	Exports to the EC	Annual % Increase	Imports from the EC	Annual % Increase	Balance	Cover ratio
1973	4.872	+ 31.9	3.193	+61.2	+ 1.679	153
1974	6.465	+ 32.7	4.020	+25.9	+ 2.445	161
1975	6.012	− 7.0	3.411	− 15.1	+ 2.601	176
1976	7.977	+ 32.7	3.651	+ 7.0	+ 4.326	218
1977	9.831	+ 23.2	4.233	+ 15.9	+ 5.598	232
1978	11.996	+ 22.0	6.106	+ 44.2	+ 5.890	196
1979	13.444	+ 12.1	7.656	+ 25.4	+ 5.788	176
1980	17.195	+ 27.9	7.878	+ 2.9	+ 9.317	218
1981	18.894	+ 9.9	8.552	+ 8.6	+ 10.341	221
1982	17.064	− 9.7	7.560	− 11.6	+ 9.504	226
1983	18.523	+ 8.5	8.120	+ 7.4	+ 10.403	228

Source: Press and Information Service, EC Delegation, Tokyo: *EC Background Note, Japan and the European Community: A Stocktaking*, April 1984, page 19.

TABLE 3
Japanese business representatives to the United States and Europe, and US and European business representatives to Japan for long-term business stays

Source: Information Centre of the Missio of Japan to the European Communities, Brussels: *News and Views from Japan*, No. 242, 9 December 1985, page 5.

Note 1: Those who are permitted to engage in trade, or in business or investment activities in Japan, with visas for stays of up to three years.

Source: Annual Immigration Control Statistics, Ministry of Justice (Japan).

	1975	1980	1981	1982	1983	1984	1985
				Europeans and Americans to Japan Entries for long-term businesss stays (Note 1)			
United States	7,813	5,393	4,770	4,905	4,832	4,675	4,336
Canada	300	243	226	232	145	126	204
Belgium	55	7	6	4	8	7	96
Denmark	11	37	26	21	25	30	16
France	223	220	148	197	159	150	186
FRG	297	202	164	196	146	195	687
Ireland	8	53	53	53	33	34	6
Italy	7	11	11	15	22	12	111
Luxembourg	0	1	0	0	0	0	0
Holland	279	167	198	169	172	192	127
UK	464	467	509	493	422	466	513
Greece	1	1	3	8	1	4	15
EC TOTAL	1,345	1,166	1,118	1,156	998	1,090	1,757
TOTAL	9,458	6,802	6,114	6,293	5,965	5,891	6,297

	Japanese to US and Europe Departures for stationing at overseas branches				
	1980	1981	1982	1983	1984
	10,505	10,224	10,580	11,850	14,841
	582	553	552	534	708
Belgium	446	418	459	530	649
Denmark	21	22	20	20	24
France	632	677	775	736	863
FRG	1,758	1,704	1,827	1,945	2,458
Ireland	25	32	40	28	24
Italy	290	313	320	386	438
Luxembourg	14	27	18	13	26
Holland	430	444	421	468	579
UK	2,050	2,080	2,253	2,358	3,192
Greece	119	103	117	107	108
EC TOTAL	5,785	5,820	6,250	6,591	8,361
	16,872	16,597	17,382	18,975	23,910

DOCUMENT 1 MOTION FOR A RESOLUTION ON TRADE RELATIONS BETWEEN THE EEC AND JAPAN AGREED BY THE COMMITTEE ON EXTERNAL ECONOMIC RELATIONS (of the European Parliament). Agreed 13 May 1981.

Source: European Communities, European Parliament, Working Documents 1981-1982 3 June 1981 Document 1-240/81. English Edition, PE 68.474/fin. pp.5-9

The European Parliament

• concerned by the persistent and increasing deficit in the Community's balance of trade with Japan.

• aware that this deficit, although comparatively small in the context of the Community's overall trade figures implies a severe threat to the Community in certain specific sectors, particularly in manufacturing industry.

• convinced that a reduction of the present trade imbalance would contribute towards a better overall understanding between the Community and Japan which would go further than purely commercial considerations and in turn lead to closer cooperation in fields such as development aid, security, monetary stability, energy conservation, and the supply of raw materials.

• recognising that it is in Japan's interest to work towards greater understanding with the Community in view of her vulnerability both in terms of national security and energy supplies.

• recognising that the problem is one which can primarily be satisfactorily resolved by increasing the competitiveness of European products vis-à-vis the Japanese in all markets and stressing therefore the need for greater effort by European industry in this respect.

• acknowledging the risk that protectionist measures may be taken by individual Member States, with resultant serious consequences not only for EEC/Japan commercial relations but also for inter-Community and world trade, and convinced that this can be averted by a greater degree of understanding by Japan of the problems that the present trade deficit poses both economically and politically for the Community.

- welcomes the fact that the Council of Ministers at their meeting of 17 February 1981 have taken positive steps to create a Community strategy towards Japan.
- recognising that the effective resolution of the problems created by the deficit in the balance of trade between the Community and Japan can best be achieved by the formulation by the Commission of a vigorous common Community trade policy towards Japan, including —

    a) closer cooperation and improved efficiencies within European industries,

    b) working together to eliminate both tariff and non-tariff barriers,

    c) encouragement of efforts by European exporters to secure a greater share of the Japanese market,

    d) reciprocity in banking and investment facilities,

    e) quantifiable self-restraint in exports by Japan in specific sectors, and a substantial increase in its imports from the Community.

- realising that unless there is an effective resolution to the deficit in trade, then pressures upon Member State Governments could force the Council of Ministers to take stringent action against Japan,
- having regard to the Motion for a Resolution tabled by Sir Fred WARNER and others (Doc. 1-966/80).
- having regard to the report of the Committee on External Economic Relations (Doc. 1-240/81).

1. REQUESTS the Council and the Commission of the European Communities to ensure that all negotiations with Japan will be conducted firmly and constructively and be based not only on an understanding of the needs of the Community but also of those of Japan and the USA who together form the world's three most significant trading groups and on whose effective cooperation any lasting global trade arrangements must depend;

2. CALLS ON the Council and Commission to ensure that any agreement concluded will provide for reciprocal measures on the part of Japan in respect of any concessions which may be granted by the Community to Japan;

3. URGES the Commission:–

(a) to continue its efforts to ensure the harmonisation of trade policy measures taken by individual Member States and also to ensure that the Community will speak 'with one voice' through the Commission in its dealings with Japan.

(b) to ensure, with respect to the Community's competition policy, that the relevant clauses of the Treaties (Articles 85 to 94) are not applied with the result that industry within the Community is penalised to the advantage of industry from third countries, including Japan;

(c) to negotiate, with Japan, specific quantifiable restraints in respect of the export of sensitive, or potentially sensitive, products to the Community. This will have to be a continuous process which will require close cooperation, at Community level, not only between Commission and Member States but also between the Commission and representatives of European industry;

(d) to make clear to Japan that any failure to abide by the restraints must lead to counter-measures on behalf of the Community;

(e) to be prepared, where it can be established that non-tariff barriers to trade exist, to introduce, at Community level, reciprocal measures within the framework of the GATT; recommends in this context that the Commission should be endowed with adequate funds to institute a service to investigate allegations of concealed protectionism, recognising that industry itself may find difficulty in dealing with such protectionism;

(f) to be prepared to accept the need, if necessary, to make existing regulations and directives regarding 'type approval' of manufactured articles, particularly motor vehicle parts, mandatory rather than permissive;

(g) to intensify its existing programme for informing European businessmen and industrialists, including those from medium and small-sized businesses and European trade union representatives on the best means of penetrating the Japanese market, with the full cooperation of the Council to make the appropriate financial means available to this end, and to enlist the full cooperation of the Japanese in this endeavour;

(h) to take steps to ensure that any agreement with Japan will include provisions ensuring full reciprocity of banking and investment facilities between the two partners; any such investments, whether on a wholly-owned or joint shareholding basis must have written agreements to ensure that a substantial percentage of components or materials used in production are sourced locally and that research and development resources are introduced as a result in order to promote employment possibilities and financial expansion in the area or region concerned:

(i) to set up a joint EEC/Japan Investment Bureau to facilitate and to encourage appropriate investment from either side. The rôle of such an Investment Bureau should include that of coordinating and extending joint undertakings between Japanese and Community countries in third countries;

4. URGES the representatives of European industry, wherever appropriate in consultation with the Commission, to cooperate closely in such fields as marketing and Research and Development and rationalisation in order to find not only the best means of penetrating the Japanese market but also of achieving viable competitiveness with respect to both Community and third country markets;

5. ASKS the Japanese for their part:–
(a) to take concrete steps to eliminate non-tariff barriers to trade, whether intentional or otherwise;

(b) to facilitate investment and banking facilities for Community countries;

(c) to accept the necessity for full cooperation with the Community in working towards monetary stabilisation by working towards monetary cooperation between those industrialised countries with convertible currencies, including the European Monetary System as a bloc, and the yen;

*(d) to cooperate with the Member States of the Community in working towards the reinvestment of the profits of the oil producing countries;

(e) to cooperate fully with the Community in accepting specific quantifiable restraints in respect of certain particularly sensitive sectors while at the same time demonstrating its willingness to accept a reasonable level of imports of manufactured goods from the Community;

(f) to cooperate with the Community in order to coordinate attitudes towards the other EEC trading partners;

6. CONSIDERS that the links between the Parliament and the Japanese Diet should be strengthened and the present exchanges intensified not only in the light of the good understanding and results so far achieved but also in order to bring about a greater political awareness of the problems which the present trade deficit pose;

7. INSTRUCTS its President to forward this resolution to the Commission and the Council and, for information, to the Government of Japan.

DOCUMENT 2 'EXTERNAL ECONOMIC MEASURES' Agreed by the Ministerial Conferencee for Economic Measures (Japan), 16 December 1981.
Source: The Japan-EC Study Group (ed.), *50 Questions and Answers, Japan's Economy and Japan-EC Trade,* Japan Times, Tokyo, 1982, pp. 55-57.

The Ministerial Conference for Economic Measures decided on 2 October of this year on its 'Economic Policy Management and Tentative Estimate of the Economic outlook' setting forth the four basic directions of price stability, recovery in balanced domestic demand, promotion of measures for recession-beset industries, and balanced expansion of trade.

However, in looking at the subsequent trends in the Japanese economy, the continuing stagnation in domestic demand persists and the current account is tending to surplus.

At the same time, the countries of the world, overall, have yet to recover from the second oil crisis, and many countries in Europe and North America in particular, face the problems of inflation and unemployment.

In view of this situation, Japan, for its part, seeking to promote the maintenance and strengthening of free trade principles, will make still greater efforts as noted below towards the objective of balanced expansion of world trade with emphasis on the recovery of domestic demand.

I. MEASURES FOR FURTHER OPENING THE MARKET

1. *Improvement of Import Testing Procedures, etc.*

In light of the intermediate report of the Trade Conference (Committee for Manufactured Goods Import Measures) and other studies, the Ministries and Agencies concerned will conduct a review of the procedures for domestic testing, etc. and put together by the end of January next year specific measures for their improvement with a view to promoting imports and in principle bringing them in line with international standards. For those which require legal amendments, the necessary amendments are to be submitted to the next Ordinary Session of the Diet.

Import testing, etc. should be conducted in a proper manner with due consideration to the aim of further opening the market.

2. *Easing of Import Restrictions*

While considering those products of interest to other countries, a review is to be made, as appropriate, of residual import restrictions. The results of this review will be reported to the Ministeial Conference for Economic Measures.

3. *Lowering of Tariff Rates*

A decision will be made soon on implementing across-the-board reduction of tariff rates two years ahead of the scheduled staging in the Tokyo Round Agreements and on reducing the tariff on whisky, etc. commensurately.

II. IMPORT PROMOTION MEASURES

1. *Implementation of Foreign Currency Lending for Emergency Imports*

Foreign currency lending based on current international interest rates will be introduced as a temporary measure with respect to the imports of important goods conducive to easing of trade frictions, while paying due attention to the exchange rate of the yen, etc.

2. *Promotion of Stockpiling, etc.*
 (i) The Government-owned oil stocks will be increased by approximately 1.5 million kilolitres in FY 1982.
 (ii) Necessary measures will be taken in order to promote private stockpiling of rare metals.

(iii) Foreign-grown grains will also be used in implementing the KR Food Aid Budget.

3. *Dispatch of Import Missions, Holding of Product Exhibitions, etc.*
In cooperation with the private sector, the dispatch of import missions, holding of product exhibitions, joint sponsoring of international symposiums, etc. will be positively promoted. Efforts will also be made to implement the statement 'On the Expansion of Manufactured Imports', utilising the Trade Conference (Committee for Manufactured Goods Import Measures).

III. EXPORT POLICY
With the basic policy of balanced expansion in trade, efforts will be made to avoid excessive concentrations of exports of specific products. In line with this policy, appropriate care will be taken in the future handling of measures currently being taken.

IV. INDUSTRIAL COOPERATION POLICY
Industrial cooperation with the EC countries, etc. will be positively promoted in such forms as exchange of investment, technology exchange, joint technology research and development, cooperation in third-country markets, etc.

V. ECONOMIC COOPERATION POLICY
Efforts will be made to fully implement the Medium-Term Target on Official Development Assistance (ODA) decided upon in January of this year.

DOCUMENT 3 'LUNCHEON ADDRESS TO THE NIHON PRESS CLUB' by Gaston E. Thorn, President of the Commission of the European Communities, 11 May 1984 (Extracts).
Source: Press and Information Service, EC Delegation, Tokyo: *EC News, May 1984 PR 84/5 (E), Embargo: 11 May, 14.30.*

But I did not come only to praise Japan. I came also to invite your country to assume to the full the obligations which are now the inescapable corollary of her achievements. Greatness always brings servitude. Success carries with it its own responsibilities. I will give two examples, one in regard to North-South cooperation and development, the other in regard to trade and the international economic system as a whole. Both of them call for a greater degree of international burden-sharing by Japan.

As regards the North-South dimension and the requirements of the developing countries, particularly the most needy among them, I would say only this. The Community, for historical and political as well as economic reasons, is ahead of its major OECD partners. Although accounting for only one third of the total GNP of OECD countries, we provide nearly half of total OECD official development aid. In 1982, our total European aid effort in dollars was four times that of Japan and one-and-a-half times that of the US. The size of the grant element in our aid and the level of disbursement were also high in that year. We acknowledge what Japan is doing, not only in bilateral aid, but also multilaterally in helping the World Bank to finance development. But we invite Japan to do much more, in relation to its economic stature.

Next, the international economic system. Leaving aside the high volume of trade transacted between the EC countries, the Community as a whole accounts for over 17% of world exports; the corresponding figure for Japan is around 9%. So we Europeans have a vested interest in favour of free trade and against protectionism. We also took (in 1982) nearly 17% of world imports, to the value of $320 billion. The corresponding figures for Japan were 7% and £132 billion. Our imports of energy are high – higher by half than yours for example. But when it comes to imports of manufactures, ours represent two-fifths of total imports, yours only one-fifth. The figures show that far from being protectionist the Community is in fact the largest open market in the world.

One of the things which we Europeans hope for from Japan is a significantly greater contribution to the main stream of the international trading order by means of a higher level of imports, notably of manufactures, and of a home market open in practice as well as theory to full two-way trade, not only for goods but also for services. In this way, the traditional autarchy of the Japanese economy can progressively give way to the interdependence and complementarity which characterise the economic relations prevailing elsewhere in the OECD area. The structural imbalances and surpluses associated with Japan, and which have imposed such strains on the open multilateral system, will be thereby alleviated. While I am familiar with the difficulties and constraints in this country, I believe that appropriate solutions can and will be found. What is clearly required is a fundamental change of Japanese attitude. I have confidence in Prime Minister Nakasone and his Cabinet colleagues to do all that is reasonably within their power to serve this general objective. The most recent package of market-opening measures is a further step in the right direction. What matters is not the means but the end, not the measures themselves but the concrete results to which they are intended to lead. I have already pointed out that the Community is a world leader in terms of the volume and percentage of world trade and aid. But in industrial, scientific and technological matters also, where the Community has a traditionally eminent position, we are now responding to the stimulus of international competition and economic change. Our ESPRIT programme for Community-backed research and development information technologies is advancing; so is our EC joint thermo-nuclear fusion project at Culham, to cite only two examples. In the financial macro-economic area, the European Monetary System (EMS) has proved its value in helping to promote monetary stability and convergence between national economies within the Community.

Most important of all, the Community is also a political as well as an economic entity. As befits an internationalist and outward-looking grouping, our Ten member States are moving towards the elaboration of a coherent collective foreign policy outlook on the world. The political cooperation machinery set up for this purpose has achieved significant results and can be expected to consolidate and strengthen in the years immediately ahead.

It follows from everything that I have said so far that cooperation between Japan and the Community deserved to be developed further, in the mutual interest. Japan's world rank and its stake in the international economic system require that she should contrive to pursue a global and balanced approach to her international trade relations. None of us can hope to achieve prosperity or security merely in a regional context. The geopolitical balance needed for Japan's prosperity and security requires as an integral element a prosperous and united Europe. The Community, on its side, accepts Japan as an equal partner. Europe is prepared to collaborate with Japan and where appropriate to learn from her. We are willing to develop industrial, scientific cooperation, we welcome more joint ventures, greater cross-investment, and enhanced financial and monetary cooperation. We attach importance to Japanese views on major international issues. The Community respects Japan's expertise, and her special political insights into Asian and particular Far Eastern matters. It is a fact that the Community and Japan share important joint responsibilities – both to each other and to the world at large, on geopolitical as well as on international economic grounds.

For me in my capacity as President of the European Commission, these are not abstractions, unrelated to my day-to-day realities. They are practical objectives to which I feel personally strongly committed. I am here this week to review all matters of concern to the Community and Japan with Japanese Ministers, and in particular with my friend and colleague, Mr Nakasone, picking up the threads of the valuable discussions I had with him last year at Williamsburg. Next week in Brussels, with Mr

Abe, Mr Komoto and Mr Okonogi, my colleagues in the Commission and I will be inaugurating a new series of 'Round Table' Ministerial discussions. Later the same week, I shall be taking part in foreign policy talks in Paris between Japan and Europe. Next month, I am looking forward to meeting the Japanese Prime Minister again — this time in London for the next Western Economic Summit. This amply demonstrates how close our working relations have already become, and how vital it will be to strengthen these relations yet further in the years ahead.

To Japan, we extend an invitation. You are now a full 'member' of the Club, a pillar of the Free World, and in certain respects an inspiration to us all in the West. We want to solve our problems with you, not by friction but through cooperation. We want to address ourselves to the world's problems in your company, and with your help. We believe you reciprocate that wish. Now is the time to put our partnership to the only true test – the achievement of concrete and lasting results.

DOCUMENT 4 STATEMENT OF PRIME MINISTER NAKASONE ON THE OUTLINE OF THE ACTION PROGRAMME, 30 July 1985.

Source: The Information Centre of the Mission of Japan to the European Communities, (Brussels), *News and Views from Japan,* Special Issue, 1985, pp. 1-3.

Today, the Government-Ruling Parties Joint Headquarters for the Promotion of External Economic Measures has decided 'the Outline of the Action Programme for Improved Market Access.' This is a decision on Japan's own initiative based upon our belief that Japan should assume roles and discharge responsibilities commensurate with its economic strength in order to maintain and strengthen the free trade system, the most important task for the present world economy.

The world economy today is charged with the danger of stumbling down a slope towards protectionism. In other words, the free world nations are at a crossroads, facing the crucial choice of continuing walking on the road of economic prosperity with free trade as its basis or following the path to an economic stagnation under protectionism. It was under this recognition that the advanced industrialised nations confirmed their commitment to take measures to roll back protectionism and agreed to promote the New Round of Multilateral Trade Negotiations at the Bonn Economic Summit meeting held in May this year. Having enjoyed maximum benefit from the free trade system since the last World War to become the second largest economy in the free world, Japan, recognising the present situation as an emergency, has decided on its own initiative, the policy measures to actively open up and liberalise its markets in order to cooperate with other countries and to head up front the battle against protectionism.

Considering Japan's leading stance in promoting the New Round, I made a commitment to make the Japanese market one of the most open markets in the world. To this end, I decided to make efforts to relax various regulations and to improve access to the Japanese market pursuant to the Action Programme which stands on the fundamental viewpoint of 'freedom in principle, restrictions only as exceptions.' The goal of the present decision is to achieve for the Japanese market an openness exceeding that of the international level, not only in terms of tariffs but also in terms of non-tariff aspects such as standards and certification.

For example, although the Japanese tariff level is already the lowest among those of the industrialised nations, further measures will be taken to eliminate or reduce tariff rates on 1,853 products, with due consideration to the requests of other countries.

In the field of standards and certification, drastic measures will be taken to reform 88 cases based on the results of thorough examination of as many as 40 relevant laws and regulations, in order to accept foreign test data and to introduce and expand self-certification systems. Transparency will be secured in the drafting and other processes of standards and certification, by admitting the participation of those related to foreign countries to all the advisory councils and other bodies. Furthermore, expansion of exchanges with foreign countries is intended in the field of services as well as by taking improvement measures.

In the field of government procurement also, liberation measures surpassing the internationally required level will be taken, such as improvement of contractual procedures and increase in the number of related organisations covered by procurement arrangements.

As for the revision of related laws and regulations and other follow-up measures, I reiterate my firm commitment to fully implement the intended goal, by establishing a responsible system in each ministry and agency, on top of which I will assume responsibility as the Chief of the Joint Headquarters in supervising and instructing the ministries/agencies concerned. In so doing, I intend to earnestly study and make full use of those opinions and advice to be raised through consultations with countries concerned and through the Office of Trade and Investment Ombudsman (O.T.O.) in pursuing further improvement.

While promoting the implementation of the Action Programme, I feel the need for a reformation of the Japanese people's minds to enable each consumer to act upon his own choice and responsibility and to more positively accept foreign products. I believe this will lead to wider selections for consumers and thus improving the livelihood of the Japanese people. Today, I wish to appeal anew to all the Japanese people to willingly accept foreign products. While I have called on business people to continue to export with prudence, I wish to call on them for even further efforts for the expansion of imports of manufactured products and others.

On top of these efforts, I instructed the ministries and agencies to improve organisational structures for promotion of imports, to actively provide equal oportunities of market entry for foreign products in their procurement and to actively encourage government-related institutions to import. I expect that not only the government-related organisations but also regional/local governments and even private enterprises would adopt the same measures as the Government. On the other hand, I have expectations of strengthening competitiveness of the product and intensifying sales promotion efforts on the part of suppliers of foreign manufactured products.

In order to aim at the elimination of economic friction through balanced expansion of economies, I believe efforts to expand domestic demand are required together with market liberalisation. A special working group will be organised to materialise, plan and promote this policy. Earnest study will be advanced on such various measures which were pointed out by the Report of the Advisory Committee for External Economic Issues, as deregulation (relaxing of official restrictions), spread of five-day work week practice, introduction of private sector vitality into public work projects, and review of the tax system.

Vitalisation of the industrial economies through investment exchanges is useful to the entire world economy. Local productions by direct overseas investment of Japanese enterprises vitalise the economies and increase employment of the host countries and, at the same time, bring a favourable result in balanced development of trade. While Japanese enterprises have rapidly increased their eagerness for direct overseas investment in recent years, I wish to ask the companies concerned for further efforts. In Japan, liberalisation of financial and capital markets is proceeding and the system for

Loans for Promotion of Foreign Direct Investment in Japan is well equipped. I welcome foreign investment in Japan and expect its expansion.

Economic development of developing countries is indispensable to the development of the world economy and trade. Japan will continue to expand and improve the Generalised System of Preferences centring on industrialised products with a view to assisting the export efforts by developing countries. Furthermore, while Japan has extended economic assistance meeting the needs of developing countries so as to contribute to the development of these countries, I intend to set a new Medium-Term Target for the expansion of aid, under which efforts for the steady expansion in quantity and improvement in quality of Official Development Assistance will be made.

Lastly, I wish to point out the importance of appropriate economic management and positive efforts to export to Japan on the part of Japan's trading partners in connection with the rectification of Japan's trade accounts and expansion of imports. At the same time, Japan expects that such efforts as bringing down interest rates in the US and other countries will result in an even higher valuation of the Yen, reflecting Japan's economic strength.

At the Bonn Economic Summit, all participating countries promised each other that each would seek for its own policy priorities in contributing to sustaining growth of the world economy and better-balanced expansion of international trade. Japan then set its course for further facilitating access to its markets and encouraging growth in imports and we are now on the verge of materialising these objectives. Trade can never be conducted by any single country alone. It require partners. I pray that all countries, with surplus or deficits, join their efforts to overcome the present difficult period.

DOCUMENT 5 COMMISSION COMMUNICATION TO THE COUNCIL – ANALYSIS OF THE RELATIONS BETWEEN THE COMMUNITY AND JAPAN, 15 October 1985.
Source: Commission of the European Communities, COM(85) 574 final, pp. 1-5.   *Extracts*

1. In a statement on EEC-Japan relations adopted on 19 June the Council 'invited the Commission to prepare a comprehensive review of Community/Japan relations with appropriate recommendations for action, as a basis for discussion and decision in the autumn of 1985.'

2. The Community's economic and trade relations with Japan have been a subject of mounting concern ever since a real imbalance became evident during the 1970s. An indication of the trend is provided by the import/export cover ratio, which has declined from 72.6% in 1970 through 44% in 1975 to its present level of around 35%.

The Council has been expressing its concern at this apparently inexorable trend since 1978.

The Commission, for its part, initiated a process of regular consultations with the Japanese authorities as early as 1973, hoping thereby to deal with trade problems in general and in particular to improve conditions for Community exporters to Japan.

In March 1978[1] Japan 'foresaw' a substantial rise in its manufactured imports. Some increase did occur in fact slightly in 1978 and 1979 (to 22.5%), fell to 19% in 1980 and rose again to 23.8% in 1984), though the increase fell short of what had been hoped.[2]

The other side of the equation — the concentration of Japanese exports on a number of sensitive sectors of Community industry at a time of industrial upheaval — has been causing the Council anxiety since 1980.[3] In a statement in November that year the Council stressed its 'serious concern' at the trade situation, deploring the 'inadequate penetration' of Community goods into the Japanese market and the 'concentration' of Japanese exports 'on a small number of particularly sensitive sectors'.

By this stage the Council was calling for a comprehensive joint strategy on Japan.[4] This meant a coordinated approach to the three major topics in our relations with that country: genuine opening up of the Japanese market to Community products, 'moderation' of Japanese exports of a growing number of sensitive products (starting with cars in 1980 and extending by 1982 to various electronic goods), and the evolution of balanced industrial, scientific and technical cooperation between the Community and Japan. These themes were developed not only in bilateral consultations but also in GATT and the western economic summits also addressed the problem.

Since then hardly a year has gone by without expressions of concern on the part of the council and the announcement by Japan of new market liberalisation measures. Seven liberalisation 'packages' have been unveiled since January 1982, plus the 'three-year action programme' announced on 30 July this year.

Although the action programme sets out some new principals in relation to standards and certification of products, such as the principle that 'freedom should be the rule and intervention by the authorities the exception,' its translation into concrete realities at the level of regulations and procedures will be phased over three years and for certain areas continues to be characterised by uncertainty and obscurity. In any case, no amount of tinkering with the bureaucratic formalities can produce import growth in short order, and it remains to be seen whether legal or administrative rule changes will be accompanied by the necessary changes of attitude and behaviour on the part of the officials who have to implement them, or of the Japanese business community in general. Finally a certain number of requests put forward by the Commission have not been taken into account.

So far, there has been no real turnaround in the trade figures. A certain moderation of Japanese exports of sensitive products has been observed but new products have come on to the market. The volume of Community manufactured exports to Japan is still small, though its exports of semi-manufactures (non-ferrous metals and chemicals) are on the increase. There has been some moderation of Japan's exports of sensitive products. The rate of growth of the Community's trade deficit has slowed but it reached £12 billion in 1984. In these circumstances, even assuming 10% annual growth in EEC exports and no change in Japan's, it would take 13 years to restore the balance.

3. As we hope to make clear, the 'Japanese problem' has a number of characteristic features:

• the crux of the problem for foreign exporters of manufactured goods to Japan is not so much visible import barriers such as tariffs or quantitative restrictions, which with a number of exceptions are generally modest, but the protracted and unpredictable technical certification and registration procedures and above all the habits and attitudes bred of Japan's vertically and horizontally integrated industrial, commercial and financial groups;

• these features of the Japanese system are undoubtedly changing, but progress is slow, and in addition the government's macro-economic policy acts as a constraint on the growth of domestic demand; this is an area where it is difficult, if not counterproductive, for foreign governments to intervene – it is up to the Japanese Government and the country's businessmen to accelerate the pace of change;

• while Japan's various trading partners, whether developed or developing, may be more or less competitive among themselves, they all by and large face similar difficulties in penetrating the Japanese market. To put it another way, the accumulated current account and trade imbalances, with no prospect of relief in sight, are dangerous because they threaten the whole operation of the multilateral trade and payments system. Simply to set the $150 billion estimated US trade deficit for 1985 against the estimated $40 million Japanese surplus is to measure the almost intolerable strains such imbalances impose on the multilateral system.

4. While this Communication is intended to convey a full picture of the whole spectrum of EEC-Japanese relations, we feel it appropriate to concentrate on the key question of economic and trade relations.

5. As a follow-up to Prime Minister Nakasone's visit to the Commission on 19 July, there are plans for a meeting of a group of Members of the Commission and their opposite numbers in the Japanese Government to be held on 18 November.

The President of the Commission is also intended to pay an official visit to Japan in January of next year.

The next western summit, due to take place in Tokyo next May, will in any case provide an opportunity to exert fresh top-level pressure on the Japanese Government.

6. Accordingly, the Commission intends to follow up the present essentially analytic Communication with a second Communication containing recommendations for action based on the outcome of discussions in the Council and the findings reported by Members of the Commission on their return from Tokyo.

1 The Ushiba Declaration of 24 March 1978.
2. In 1984 manufactures accounted for 44% of Community imports, yet the Community too has to import a substantial proportion of its fuel and raw material requirements.
3. Statement of 25 November 1980.
4. Statement of 7 February 1978.

APPENDIX 1
PRIME MINISTERS OF JAPAN SINCE THE RESTORATION OF JAPANESE SOVEREIGNTY 28 April 1952

Yoshida Shigeru	15 October 1948 – 10 December 1954
Hatoyama Ichirō	10 December 1954 – 23 December 1956
Ishibashi Tanzan	23 December 1956 – 25 February 1957
Kishi Nobusuke	25 February 1957 – 19 July 1960
Ikeda Hayato	19 July 1960 – 9 November 1964
Satō Eisaku	9 November 1964 – 7 July 1972
Tanaka Kakuei	7 July 1972 – 9 December 1974
Miki Takeo	9 December 1974 – 24 December 1976
Fukuda Takeo	24 December 1976 – 7 December 1978
Ōhira Masayoshi	7 December 1978 – 18 July 1980
Suzuki Zenkō	18 July 1980 – 26 November 1982
Nakasone Yasuhiro	26 November 1982 –

APPENDIX 2
PRESIDENTS OF THE COMMISSION OF THE EUROPEAN ECONOMIC COMMUNITY (7 JANUARY 1958 – 30 JUNE 1967) AND OF THE EUROPEAN COMMUNITIES, FROM 1ST JULY 1967.

Walter Hallstein (Federal Republic of Germany)	7 January 1958 – 30 June 1967
Jean Rey (Belgium)	1 July 1967 – 30 June 1970
Franco Maria Malfatti (Italy)	1 July 1970 – 21 March 1972
Sicco Mansholt (Netherlands)	22 March 1972 – 5 January 1973
Francois-Xavier Ortoli (France)	5 January 1973 – 4 January 1977
Roy Jenkins (United Kingdom)	6 January 1977 – 5 January 1981
Gaston F. Thorn (Luxembourg)	6 January 1981 – 5 January 1985
Jacques Delors (France)	6 January 1985 –

APPENDIX 3
JAPANESE MINISTERS OF FOREIGN AFFAIRS SINCE THE RESTORATION OF SOVEREIGNTY, 28 APRIL 1952.

Yoshida Shigeru	16 February 1949 – 30 April 1952
Okazaki Katsuo	30 April 1952 – 10 December 1954
Shigemitsu Mamoru	10 December 1954 – 23 December 1956
Kishi Nobusuke	23 December 1956 – 10 July 1957
Fujiyama Aiichirō	10 July 1957 — 19 July 1960
Kosaka Zentarō	19 July 1960 – 18 July 1962
Ōhira Masayoshi	18 July 1962 – 18 July 1964
Shiina Etsusaburō	18 July 1964 – 3 December 1966
Miki Takeo	3 December 1966 – 30 November 1968
Aichi Kiichi	30 November 1968 – 5 July 1971
Fukuda Takeo	5 July 1971 – 7 July 1972
Ōhira Masayoshi	7 July 1972 – 16 July 1974
Kimura Toshio	18 July 1974 – 9 December 1974
Miyazawa Kiichi	9 December 1974 – 15 September 1976
Kosaka Zentarō	15 September 1976 – 24 December 1976

Hatoyama Iichirō	24 December 1976 – 28 November 1977
Sonada Sunao	28 November 1977 – 9 November 1979
Ōkita Saburō	9 November 1979 – 17 July 1980
Itō Masayoshi	17 July 1980 – 18 May 1981
Sonoda Sunao	18 May 1981 – 30 November 1981
Sakurauchi Yoshio	30 November 1981 – 27 November 1982
Abe Shintarō	27 November 1982 –

APPENDIX 4
COMMISSIONERS FOR EXTERNAL RELATIONS OF THE EUROPEAN ECONOMIC COMMUNITY (JANUARY 1958 – JULY 1967) AND OF THE EUROPEAN COMMUNITIES (FROM 1 JULY 1967).

Jean Rey (Belgium)	7 January 1958 – 1 July 1967
Edoardo Martino (Italy)	1 July 1967 – 30 June 1970
Ralf Dahrendorf (Federal Republic of Germany)	1 July 1970 – 5 January 1973
Sir Christopher Soames (United Kingdom)	6 January 1973 – 5 January 1977
Wilhelm Haferkamp (Federal Republic of Germany)	6 January 1977 – 5 January 1985
Willy de Clercq (Belgium)	6 January 1985 –

APPENDIX 5
JAPANESE AMBASSADORS TO THE EUROPEAN ECONOMIC COMMUNITY, THE EUROPEAN COAL AND STEEL COMMUNITY AND EURATOM (DECEMBER 1959 – JUNE 1967) AND TO THE COMMISSION OF THE EUROPEAN COMMUNITIES (FROM JULY 1967 TO THE PRESENT).*

Wajima Eiji	24 July 1957 – 16 January 1961
Shimoda Takezō	16 January 1961 – 10 December 1963
Yukawa Morio	10 December 1963 – 6 November 1967
Otabe Kinichi	6 November 1967 – 23 February 1970
Abe Isao	23 February 1970 – 12 March 1975
Nishibori Masahiro	12 March 1975 – 18 March 1979
Kagawa Takaaki	18 March 1979 – 24 January 1983
Kagami Hideo	24 January 1983 –

*Until March 1979 the Japanese Ambassador to Belgium also acted as Ambassador to the three European institutions. From 2 April 1979, a separate Ambassador was appointed to the Commission of the European Communities.

APPENDIX 6
HEADS OF THE EUROPEAN COMMUNITY'S DELEGATION IN TOKYO, SINCE ITS OPENING ON 31 MAY 1974.

Wolfgang Ernst (Federal Republic of Germany) (31 May 1974 – 23 October 1978)
Leslie Fielding (United Kingdom) (24 October 1978 – 1 December 1982)
Laurens Jan Brinkhorst (Netherlands) (4 December 1982 –   )